Nurtured by Love

Nurtured by Love

The Classic Approach to Talent Education

Second Edition

Shinichi Suzuki

Translated by Waltraud Suzuki

Illustrated

An Exposition-Banner Book

EXPOSITION PRESS   SMITHTOWN, NEW YORK

First Printing, 1983
Second Printing, 1984

SECOND EDITION

© 1983 by Shinichi Suzuki
First Edition (hardcover only) Published 1969. Nineteenth Printing 1981

Library of Congress Catalog Card Number: 82-90710

ISBN 0-682-49930-7 (hardcover)
ISBN 0-682-49910-2 (paperback)
Printed in the United States of America

To my wife with gratitude

ACKNOWLEDGMENTS

I wish to record my deep gratitude to Mrs. Masako Kobayashi for her help in reading the Japanese, and to Miss D. Guyver Britton for so kindly going through the English manuscript.

WALTRAUD SUZUKI
Translator

PREFACE

Talent is no accident of birth.

In today's society a good many people seem to have the idea that if one is born without talent, there is nothing he can do about it; they simply resign themselves to what they consider to be their "fate."Consequently they go through life without living it to the full or ever knowing life's true joy. That is man's greatest tragedy.

We are born with natural ability to learn. A newborn child adjusts to his environment in order to live, and various abilities are acquired in the process. My thirty years' experience has proved over and over again that this is true. Many children grow up in an environment that stunts and damages them, and it is assumed that they were born that way; they themselves believe it too. But they are wrong.

An undesirable, disagreeable adult is one who was brought up wrong: so it is with a person unable to do good work. I believe that most readers will agree with me. So-called fate, of course, we cannot deny. We can do nothing about our being born into this world, nor about our having to die sooner or later.

Good or bad, however, once born we must live with ourselves until the day we die. There arises, then, the inevitable question of how to live. If our ability was not nurtured properly, we have to develop it ourselves. Instead of being defeated by misfortune, we have to make something good of our lives. There is no reason to give up in discouragement; it is possible for every person to improve himself.

That is why I wrote this book.

In it I tell how to develop a person's aptitude; how a mediocre child was turned into a noble human being and an excellent musician. Using examples, I explain how to change a person with stunted ability into a talented one, a mediocre person into an exceptional

ix

one. Questions are answered as to how the reader may relate this to himself. Theory is dispensed with and the emphasis is on how to put all this into practice. I relate happy examples and episodes from teaching violin the Talent Education way.

A living tree brings forth buds; on each branch blooms lovely flowers. It is the splendid course of nature. Man, I believe, should follow Mother Nature and bring forth fruit.

What is man's ultimate direction in life? It is to look for love, truth, virtue, and beauty. That goes for you, for me, for everyone. If this book can be of help, even a little, I cannot say how happy it will make me.

Shinichi Suzuki

Nurtured by Love

INTRODUCTION

All Japanese children speak Japanese

Oh—why, Japanese children can all speak Japanese! The thought suddenly struck me with amazement. In fact, all children throughout the world speak their native tongues with the utmost fluency. Any and every Japanese child—all speak Japanese without difficulty. Does that not show a startling talent? How, by what means, does this come about? I had to control an impulse to shout my joy over this discovery.

The children of Osaka speak the difficult Osaka dialect. We are unable to imitate the Tohoku dialect, but the Tohoku children speak it. Isn't that something of an accomplishment? But no one else I mentioned it to seemed the slightest bit impressed. It was just taken for granted; people in general think that the ability children display is inborn. At my excitement, half of my listeners were startled, and others just thought me absurd. Nevertheless, my discovery actually had great significance; it made me realize that any child is able to display highly superior abilities if only the correct methods are used in training. This happened about thirty years ago, when I was thirty-three or thirty-four years old. Following up the thought that struck me so forcibly on that day, and trying to find a solution, soon became the basic purpose of my life.

I think it was around 1931 or 1932, when I was teaching violin at the Imperial Conservatory to a class of mostly young men, that a father came to our home accompanied by his four-year-old son. The boy is now a world-famous musician: Toshiya Eto.

How does this surprising fact come about?

The father asked me to teach his son violin. At that time I didn't know how to train such a small child, or what to teach him. I didn't

1

have such experience. What kind of violin training would be good for a four-year-old? I thought about it from morning to night.

The answer came from my discovery.

At that time three of my brothers and I had just formed the Suzuki Quartet. One day when we were practicing at the house of my younger brother, it hit me like a flash: all Japanese children speak Japanese! This thought struck me like a flash of light in a dark night. Since they all speak Japanese so easily and fluently, there must be a secret; and this must be training. Indeed, all children everywhere in the world are brought up by a perfect educational method: their mother tongue. Why not apply this method to other faculties? I felt I had made a tremendous discovery. If a child cannot do his arithmetic, it is said that his intelligence is below average. Yet he can speak the difficult Japanese language—or his own native language—very well. Isn't this something to ponder and think about? In my opinion the child who cannot do arithmetic is not below average in intelligence; it is the educational system that is wrong. His ability or talent simply has not been developed properly. It is astonishing that no one discovered this before, although the situation clearly has existed throughout human history.

Ability training is the secret

1. If the mother-tongue method of education were used in schools today, the results would far surpass those obtained by present methods. For instance, we often hear: "Here is a child who is not very bright; he was born with low intelligence." But how do we account for the splendid capacity of children to speak Japanese? Do we search for a better method of training? Furthermore, a child is judged only from five or six years of age on. Nobody seems to care what happened before—what kind of education the child had from early infancy.

2. All children skillfully reared reach a high educational level but such rearing must start from the day of birth. Here, to my mind, lies the key to the fuller development of man's potentials and abilities.

When I was asked to teach four-year-old Toshiya, I thought—and kept thinking—How? Finally the mother-tongue method occurred to me and I felt that it contained all that was necessary. For thirty years now I have been pleading with people to believe that *all* children can be well educated, and not to turn away those who drop behind in learning. I named my method Talent Education, and began an educational movement in which children dropping behind or struggling to get along are not turned away. The day of my startling discovery became for me the starting point in my search for human potentials. And how did I fare? With glances back at the past and full of hope for the future, I should like to tell the story.

NURTURED BY LOVE

Planting the seed of ability

A seed needs time and stimulation . . .

In our Tokyo Shinagawa branch, headed by Mr. Miyazawa, was a little parakeet, the pet of tiny children who went there for their violin lessons. When Mr. and Mrs. Miyazawa bought the bird, the couple taught it to say in Japanese: "I am Peeko Miyazawa, I am Peeko Miyazawa." The bird, in his high-pitched voice, later said to the children what it had happened to hear: "Peeko is a good little bird, Peeko is a good little bird." According to Mr. Miyazawa, you must begin training a bird soon after birth. In the beginning you must have much perseverance, energy, and patience. In order to make the parakeet speak, and develop its ability, it is necessary to repeat the same word over and over again. Just when you think it is useless, despair, and want to give up, you are finally rewarded with some results.

At first the name Peeko was repeated to the bird about fifty times daily; that made three thousand times in two months. Then, at last, the little bird began to say "Peeko." If this word had not been coached so assiduously every day, the bird would never have had the "talent" or "ability" to say it. By daily training the knowledge was implanted, then the ability had to be developed until the time was ripe. Preparation, time, and environment came together as stimulants. We don't see the seed that is planted in the ground, but water, temperature, light and shade act daily as stimuli; little by little there is an unseen change, up to a certain day when the sprout appears. Aren't the situations comparable?

5

With patience and repetition, the seed blossoms

Once a shoot comes out into the open, it grows faster and faster. After teaching the bird to say, by repeating it three thousand times, "Peeko," "Miyazawa" was added. This time, after having heard "Peeko Miyazawa" daily for fifteen minutes, he could say it after only two hundred times.

No doubt it is the same with a human being. Whatever he learns, the beginning will be slow until the "bud of ability" takes hold. This procedure requires time, but gradually a high ability develops. Isn't this true? To think it is hopeless or to give up because at first there are no visible results makes all the former training done with so much trouble a waste. The first "planted" ability will also wither away. It is therefore a matter of patience and repetition. If this is done—and we have watched the splendid training Peeko had—we can well understand that ability breeds ability.

Later Peeko learned various words by himself. When the children in the studio played the first tune in the Talent Education program, "Twinkle, Twinkle, Little Star," Peeko learned to sing it in rhythm with his little voice. This shows that talent develops talent and that the planted seed of ability grows with ever increasing speed. Mr. Miyazawa related the following episode: "It was interesting when I coughed for some days due to a cold. Peeko would say his usual 'I am Peeko Miyazawa' and then cough. The cough, of course, nobody had taught him; he added it by himself."

The coughing of the parakeet is evidence for my belief in the development of ability. Because Mr. Miyazawa could train a little bird like this, I have great respect for his ability to train and educate children.

A tiny baby responds with joy to a familiar melody

The following incident happened fourteen or fifteen years ago one spring in Ueda City, Shinshu Province.

Members of Talent Education met at the house of an acquaintance for some pleasant conversation. The children of Mrs. Shimada and Mrs. Kiuchi came in holding their small violins. "Well, shall we have some music?" someone suggested, and, as always, the children happily began to play the various pieces in unison and gave us a concert. Just in front of me sat Mrs. Kiuchi, holding a baby in her arms. I inquired its age and was told that the infant, named Hiromi, was just five months old. Hiromi's sister, Atsumi, six years old, was daily practicing at that time the Vivaldi A-minor concerto, as well as listening to the record every day. So Hiromi grew up hearing this music daily from the very beginning. I was anxious to know what effect this had on a five-month-old baby, so I announced that I would like to play something, and stood up with my violin. When everybody was quiet, I started playing a minuet by Bach. While I played, my eyes did not leave Hiromi's face. The five-month-old already knew the sound of the violin well, and her eyes shone while she listened to this piece that she was hearing for the first time. A little while later I switched from the minuet to the Vivaldi A minor concerto—music that was played and heard continuously in her home. I had no sooner started the piece when an amazing thing happened.

Hiromi's expression suddenly changed. She smiled and laughed, and turned her happy face to her mother, who held her in her arms. "See—that's *my* music," she unmistakably wanted to tell her mother. Soon again, her face turned in my direction, and she moved her body up and down in rhythm. This baby, just five months old, had shown that she knew the melody of the Vivaldi A-minor concerto. In this way, inspiration and interest are acquired involuntarily by an infant from everything he sees and hears, like a seed that is planted. This is what molds—forms—the character. That, I thought, was clear from what I had seen.

It is a frightening fact. By no means only words or music, but everything, good or bad, is absorbed.

Four years later at a big concert in Matsumoto, there were 150 children on the stage with their small violins. They were playing the Vivaldi A-minor concerto.

"Who is that four- or five-year-old girl in the center of the front row?'' I asked. This child was putting her whole heart and soul into her playing, and her posture was excellent as she happily swayed with the rhythm.

"That is Hiromi Kiuchi from Ueda."

It was the same child. Indeed, I remembered the five-month-old baby taking real pleasure in natural training, and there she was with her ability nicely developed.

Such children are the fruit of training and environment

Ten years later I received a letter, with some music attached, from Hiromi, who was then a junior-high-school student: "Dear Professor: I wrote this poem and composed the music of this song. There was a contest for all junior high schools throughout Japan in verse writing and composition. My song was accepted and won first place."

It takes a great deal of artistic sense to write poetry and music. Remembering the baby held in its mother's arms listening to my playing of the Vivaldi concerto and joyfully matching the rhythm with the movements of her body, I am convinced that this beautiful talent and admirable humanity were trained by the method the parents used for her education.

Atsumi and Hiromi, born ordinary children, were indeed fortunate to be reared like this.

Every single human being's personality—his ability, his way of thinking and feeling—is carved and chiseled by training and environment. It shows in each person's face and eyes. His whole character becomes visible. The stamp of history changes day by day, matching the steps of man's living. This is life's delicate working.

Later it will be explained whether one will or will not cope with the rising question of how and in what way to live. But now, for a little while, I will continue to speak on the matter of concern: how to grow up and how to bring up.

Talent is not inherited

The first month in a nightingale's life determines its fate.. . .

I had always thought that a nightingale's incomparable song was instinctive or inherited. But it is not so. Nightingales to be used as pets are taken as fledglings from nests of wild birds in the spring. As soon as they lose their fear and accept food, a "master bird" is borrowed that daily sings its lovely song, and the infant bird listens for a period of about a month. In this way the little wild bird is trained by the master bird. This method has been used in Japan since olden times. The best environment is furnished for training the birds. In short, it is the nightingale's "talent education." The master bird plays the role of teacher to the little bird. The pupil goes on to receive various other kinds of training, but it is most important to have a good teacher during the first month. Whether the wild bird will develop good or bad singing quality is indeed decided in the first month by the voice and tone of its teacher. It is not a matter of being born a good or a bad singer. Be it only the case of a nightingale, the life force has a wonderful power to adapt to environment. If it has a good teacher, the infant bird will, through physiological transformation, learn from experience to produce tones as beautiful as those of its teacher. But if a bird is brought to such a teacher after being raised by wild nightingales, there is always failure, as long experience has shown. This is the law of nature in shaping and forming life's potential. Isn't the example of the little nightingale a valuable hint for the development of human potential as well?

I myself believe this very strongly. For the sake of our little ones, therefore, I stress as much as I can the need to provide the best influences in rearing children.

All the world's children could be brought up singing out of tune

The shaping of life's capacity stems from the simple rule seen in the example of the nightingale. Now we will look at the forming of ability in a human being. Mothers often say to me, "I am tone-deaf," to explain that their child is the same. They think it is hereditary and that there is nothing they can do about it. But just as nightingales are not born tone-deaf, neither are human infants. On the contrary, a baby absorbs perfectly any out-of-tune pitch of its mother's lullabies. It has a marvelous ear. That's why the child will later sing in the same way. Osaka children absorb the intricate Osaka dialect in exactly the same fashion.

If a baby is brought up listening to a recording of a song out of tune, his ears will become accustomed to it, and it will be very hard for him to change later on. Thus, if we wanted to, we could make all children throughout the world tone-deaf. But it is clear that if we can do this, there is no such thing as intrinsic musical talent. This fact needs to be understood. We need to understand the importance of the ear.

In short—

1. We must study how to develop talent through education.
2. We must realize that talent, not only in music but in other fields as well, is not inherited.

Two children brought up by a wolf

Man is born without talent. People are what they are as a result of their own specific environments. The life force adapts itself to fit the environment. This is brought out clearly in a valuable work by Dr. Fumio Kida, entitled *Child Psychology*. In it Dr. Kida tells the story of two little girls brought up by a wolf.

In 1941 two professors from Denver and Yale universities received an account of a valuable piece of research. A priest in India had found two small children who had been raised by a wolf. One was about two years old and the other about seven. The younger one was named Amala, the other Kamala. The account covered nine years of observations after they were found, including photos by Father Singh. The discovery was made northwest of Calcutta in a jungle zone. (It is said that among natives in India the practice of abandoning girl babies still prevails.)

Head, breast and shoulders of both children were covered with thick hair. After it was cut, they looked like human beings.

In the wolf's cave the infants crawled on all fours, their eyes seeing clearly in the dark. Their noses were extremely sensitive. They ran fast on all fours, like a dog, and people could not overtake them. Their shoulders were wide, their legs powerful, with bent thighs that would not stretch out straight. They grasped things with their mouths, not with their hands. Food and water were taken in a doglike manner. Kamala was particularly advanced in the way of a wolf. She was not only fond of raw meat but showed a strong predilection for rotten meat. She was immune to change in temperature and did not perspire. When it was hot, she would hang out her tongue and pant like a dog. Her skin had a glassy smoothness and did not become soiled. But the palms of her hands were callused. Her head with its long and matted hair was grotesquely large. At the slightest noise her ears stood up and she became tense. It she was angered, her nostrils would flare and she would growl like a dog. If one tried to interfere while she was eating, she would bare her teeth and snarl.

During the day she slept, but as soon as the sun set her activity started. At night, just as she had done when she lived among wolves, she would howl three times at accurate intervals—at ten, one, and three o'clock. This habit had become second nature, because for years she had been howling regularly with the wolves together in a chorus. She did not stop howling during the nine years she was with human beings, but continued until she died, at the age of sixteen. Kamala's voice had neither human nor animal characteristics. The sound was peculiar, indeterminable.

Could you call this *inherited?*

A human child living among wolves and brought up by them took on their habits. To survive, man instinctively adapts himself to his surroundings. A tremendous and sublime life force works to grasp the components of our environment. I am filled with awe at the thought of this power.

The facts above show how important it is to guide children all through early life. We must give much thought as to *how* children should be reared and trained, how the development of their minds, sense, wisdom and conduct should be guided. Till now we have thought and believed that all this was inborn or inherited. I strongly recommend that we abandon such notions. What misery it was for Amala and Kamala to have been raised as they were! It came to an end when they were taken from the wolf's cave and brought into human society, but their experience proves to us the power of the living soul. In spite of being human, they both adapted very well to their condition in life, that is, to the condition of a wolf. If this high degree of power had been allowed to work in them in a civilized community with good environment, there would have been splendid educational results. As it was, scientists judged them to be idiots. I don't think they were, considering how well they adapted themselves to their surroundings. The point is it is not heredity that molds us but environment. Children live, see, and feel, and their ability develops to fit their surroundings. Of course, this hypothesis ignores heredity, which people stubbornly insist is so important.

But consider these children running around on all fours, using their mouths like dogs to grasp things between their teeth instead of using their hands, and having a desire for raw meat and a fancy for rotten food. Moreover, they were young girls; yet their shoulders and breasts were covered with thick hair. Can anyone say that this is hereditary?

Now, in our society we don't actually throw our children to the wolves. But the poor environment some have to experience soon after birth hurts and damages their developing abilities to such an extent that it is almost as bad as having been raised among wolves. To look at a school-age child with stunted or damaged abilities and say that this is inherited is a grave mistake. The destiny of children lies in the hands of their parents.

What does not exist in the environment cannot be developed

We have no way of knowing the qualities of a suckling. . . .

The faculty I know best is music. That is why I will talk about music—whether inherited gifts or qualities exist or not. It has been always thought that talent or superior qualities are inborn, or inherited. But can we test a suckling to find out whether or not such things are present? The problem is that children five or six years old and already trained are judged from there on as to their ability, superior or inferior. Yet it is the earliest stages of infancy that are critical. We should be doing research in the potential talents of suckling babes. If we are going to meet the challenges of the future, we should be fulfilling the basic needs of mankind. These are the things to study. I do the best I can, but that is not enough.

In the matter of disposition and heredity, I am convinced that it is *only* the body's physiological functioning ability that can be measured as either superior or inferior at the time of birth. From then on, *only* psychological influences are received *from the child's environment*. And it is the conditions of that environment that shape the core of his ability.

Good environmental conditions produce superior abilities

We don't have to look for specific innate abilities or talents. It is a superior environment that has the greatest effect in creating superior abilities. The cases of Hiromi Kiuchi and the nightingale and Peeko, the parakeet, all bear this out. There is no use in judging children's abilities from the training they receive five or six years *after* birth. Abilities are born and developed by the working of the vital forces of the organism as it strives to live and to adapt to its environment right in the beginning. Therefore, *the only superior quality a child can have at birth is the ability to adapt itself with more speed and sensitivity to its environment than others.*

A clever baby can become tone-deaf. It can even become a wolf. In fact, it can become just about anything, in accord with its specific environment. I firmly believe that cultural and musical aptitude does not come from within, and is not inherited, but occurs through suitable environmental conditions. It is only a question of sensitivity and adaptive speed. Therefore, to be born with excellent or superior qualities only means to be born with an ability to adapt more speedily and sensitively to one's environment. For a human being to acquire a wolf's sense and habits shows man's ability to adapt to his environment, whatever it may be. If Einstein, Goethe, and Beethoven had been born during the Stone Age, wouldn't they likewise have had only the cultural ability and education of men of the Stone Age? The converse is also true: if I were to receive a suckling babe of the Stone Age and educate him, before long he would be able to play a violin sonata by Beethoven as well as any young person of today. Again, if a child born today were to be brought up and educated in a society of five thousand years hence, he would adapt to the customs and habits of that society.

What does not exist in the cultural environment will not develop in the child

Wherever they are born—in Western countries, in the Orient, or in different districts of Africa—children are brought up according to their own particular culture. Children have to adapt to manifold environments and are brought up in superior or inferior surroundings, depending on their parents.

There is no result without cause. Wrong education and upbringing produces ugly personalities, whereas a fine upbringing and good education will bring forth superior sense and feeling, as well as nobility and purity of mind.

All children adapt the vital forces of their organism to their respective environments.

Professor N. H. Pronko of Wichita (Kansas) University came to visit me in Matsumoto several years ago. He had made experiments along these lines and found that babies brought up in different cultural environments during their first nine months adapted themselves to their respective environments. Qualities not required by any particular environment did not develop. He had published the results of his studies in America.

I cannot emphasize firmly enough and often enough how wrong it is to judge an already trained child and to say that its abilities are due to superiority or inferiority at birth. This kind of thinking should be abandoned. We must put an end to this misconception. There is no telling to what heights children can attain if we educate them properly right after birth. Should we not investigate the possibilities? Good environmental conditions and a fine education cannot help but contribute to children's welfare and happiness, as well as promising light and hope for the future of mankind.

"Will my boy amount to something?"— *an offensive question*

The mother of one of my students came one day to inquire about her son. This student had good musical sense, practiced very well, and was a superior child.

"Sensei [Professor], will my boy amount to something?" the mother asked me, just like that.

I answered laughingly, "No. He will not become 'something.' "

It seems to be the tendency in modern times for parents to entertain thoughts of this kind. It is an undisguisedly cold and calculating educational attitude. When I hear things like this, I want to reply in a joking way. But the mother was alarmed and surprised by my answer.

So I continued, "He will become a noble person through his violin playing. Isn't that good enough? You should stop wanting your child to become a professional, a good money earner. This thought is concealed in your question and is offensive. A person with a fine and pure heart will find happiness. The only concern for parents should be to bring up their children as noble human beings. That is sufficient. If this is not their greatest hope, in the end the child may take a road contrary to their expectations. Your son plays the violin very well. We must try to make him splendid in mind and heart also."

The boy who received his first lessons *from his father*

That I had started a new educational movement in violin teaching became known to various parents.

"Will you please listen to my boy's playing?" Mr. X of Nagoya City asked. He had taught his son himself. The boy was then eighteen years old and was studying the Mozart Concerto No. 5.

"Gladly," I said. "Please tell him to visit me any time."

About a month later the young man came alone to see me. Seeing the youth for the first time, I was surprised at how much he resembled his father—the tone of his voice, his Nagoya dialect, his manner of speaking, even his greeting, the same habit of both hands in front of him, his laugh too—everything just like his father, so much so, I had the illusion of speaking to Mr. X.

I asked the boy to begin playing. He took his violin out of the case, and, while tuning it, handled the bow with the same quickness and movements as his father. But that was not all. When he began to play, his posture, the movements of hands and bow, were absolutely the same as his father's. But not only that—even the shortcomings in his performance and musical sense, sometimes linking musical intervals—his tone, and various small details—all resembled his father's.

Until then I had never been so vividly impressed with how much a child adapts to his environment. The fact that he had lived in this family for eighteen years showed distinctly in the young man's behavior, sense, and feeling.

About thirty years ago little four-year-old Toshiya Eto became my first small pupil. Then came another infant pupil, Koji Toyoda. When we moved from Nagoya to Tokyo, Koji's father also moved to Tokyo.

Later, after hearing three-year-old Koji Toyoda play Dvorak's "Humoresque" and seven-year-old Toshiya Eto play a concerto, a father visited me, bringing along his three-year-old son. He asked my opinion as to whether or not his son had musical talent. If the boy was talented, he would like him to study violin.

Who can judge whether a three-year-old boy has musical talent and cultural aptitude? I told the father that talent is not inherited or inborn but has to be learned and developed, but he didn't understand me. How many such parents there are in the world!

Reflecting on the young man who grew up to be the image of his father, I think, generally speaking, that we need only look at the parents to guess what the children will be like.

The remarkable life force

The bow flies away, the mother picks it up. . . .

There are branches of Talent Education throughout Japan. Any child can enter without any test, because our principle is based on the premise that talent is not inborn, that every child acquires ability through experience and repetition.

For the sake of our children, let us educate them from the cradle to have a noble mind, a high sense of values, and splendid ability. At our institute we use violin playing to develop these qualities in children.

All teachers of our Talent Education branches follow this course. Together with parents they spare no effort in guiding children to becoming noble human beings.

The following episode took place at our Nakatsugawa City, Gifu Prefecture, branch. Among the many students there was a six-year-old girl who had had infantile paralysis; she was not able to control the right side of her body, and she had a squint in the right eye. When playing "Twinkle, Twinkle, Little Star," just as she got to the last two notes of the first phrase, her right arm and hand would involuntarily give a violent twitch, sending the bow flying out of her hand.

Mr. Yogo, the teacher, was very distressed and troubled. He told me about it and asked for advice. I simply gave the following answer: "Both teacher and parents should accept the fact and keep on." The teacher patiently went on with lessons, and every day the mother picked up the bow innumerable times. It must have been very hard for her. But the great love and persistent endeavor of both mother and teacher won out. The time came when the child was finally able to hold the bow throughout the entire piece.

A half year of endeavor and persistent effort

In the relatively short time of about six months the girl was able to play "Twinkle, Twinkle, Little Star" all the way through. Thanks to the daily training, power came back to her right hand and her ability was established.

The mother and the teacher went through this half year's ordeal together. What had looked like an impossibility became a possibility. If they had given up in despair, this ability would never have been born. An invisible, growing faculty helped to breed the new ability until finally it became visible to all. When I praised the mother for the hardships she had gone through, she said, "I thought, if only she could learn to play a little! But she dropped the bow so often that I was discouraged, and thought it was no use. Thanks to you, she now can play the whole piece and can control her hand. The child is very happy." Fortunately the little girl kept on practicing, and her right eye, which had been crossed, gradually started moving to the correct position, while at the same time she began to gain control of her right side; gradually she could move normally. In this way she recovered from the effects of her infantile paralysis and found her way back to health. All this was achieved through the therapy of her efforts in playing just one piece of music, aided by the endeavors of her mother and her teacher.

Natural ability is brought out by training

"Ability is life." My belief was proved before my eyes by the young girl with infantile paralysis.

Mankind is governed by the life force. The living soul, with a desire to go on living, displays great power in adapting itself to its environment. The human life force, by seeing and feeling its surroundings, trains itself and develops ability. This ability by further constant training overcomes difficulties and becomes a very high ability. This is the relationship between a human being and ability. The development of ability cannot be accomplished by mere thinking or theorizing, but must be accompanied by action and practice, as I shall show in another chapter. Only through action can the power of the life force be displayed. Ability develops through practice. An idle person will not develop ability. Suppose the parents of the little girl with infantile paralysis had been resigned to the fact of her illness and had done nothing about it? She would have stayed crippled. Through violin playing and memorizing the music, her brain and body were stimulated. And it was this *activity* that made the child mentally and physically sound.

Koji

In 1962, autumn came early to the Shinshu region. The foliage was beginning to turn color, when this letter arrived:

Berlin, September 1962

MY HONORED AND REVERED TEACHER:

I have just come to Berlin. When you, Professor, were here, in which neighborhood did you live? I have always dreamed of seeing this place. All the new buildings in Berlin still seem somewhat cold. But the people differ from those of rural Cologne in elegance, refinement and politeness. Yesterday I was given an audition by the Berlin Symphony Orchestra, and appointed first concertmaster. The conductor—Fricsay—ranks at present in Germany with Karajan and Kubelick. The only worry I have now is whether I am really fit to take up the position of First Violinist in such a famed orchestra.

With affection and most respectfully,

KOJI

Koji wrote me this letter on arriving in Berlin, after leaving Cologne. Reading it, I was not only filled with emotion but with surprise, as well.

Koji earns the love and respect of the musical world

It was the first time since Western music had come to Japan that a Japanese had won a position like this in Europe. It hardly seemed possible, for I know the high standing of the Berlin orchestra. To be this orchestra's representative is a most important position. The chief concertmaster a Japanese—Koji . . . !

To be able to fill this position one must have three things: (1) high musical sense, (2) superior musical performance, (3) a fine character. One must be endowed with all three together. A true artist is a person with beautiful and fine feelings, thoughts, and actions. This is the message and entreaty I hand down to my students. Koji's singleminded pursuit of art in accordance with these ideals had finally earned him the respect of his peers.

A recent letter from a member of this orchestra, Hiroko Yamada, shows the love and respect that Koji has earned in the musical world, and the importance of his position.

Koji, respected as he is by all its members, is probably the most modest and helpful person in the orchestra. I can say this because I know him well.

Koji first played on stage when my pupils gave a violin performance at the Nihon Seinenkan, in Tokyo. Toshiya Eto was then seven years old. That evening he played the Seitz Violin Concerto No. 3, accompanied by the Tokyo String Orchestra. Yoko Arimatsu, just five, also played very well. After she had finished, she shouldered her violin and ran happily off the stage. She was a charming little girl, and we all burst out laughing. And then, his 1/16-size violin in his hand, three-year-old Koji came to the stage. He played "Humoresque," while his father accompanied him on the guitar. The following day there were big photos of Koji in the main newspapers, and articles with the headings "A Genius Appears," "Brilliant," "Wonderful," and so on. Previous to the performance I had told journalists, "Talent is not inherited or inborn, but learned and trained. Genius is an honorific name given to those who are brought up and trained to high ability." I had emphasized this point and repeated it; it is indeed regrettable and disappointing that they didn't understand.

Well, this happened some thirty-five years ago.

My invaluable friends

When I undertook in Nagoya the task of teaching violin, Koji's father lived in Hamamatsu. At the beginning of 1930 we moved to

Dr. Suzuki at work

Dr. Suzuki with several of his young students

Dr. Suzuki and his wife, Waltraud

Tokyo. Soon after, Mr. Toyoda also moved to Tokyo with his whole family, and little Koji studied attentively at our house. It was a result of circumstances that he played the violin. Whether he liked it or disliked it is not the question. Precisely as all Japanese children learn the Japanese language, and learn it by heart, to like or dislike it had no bearing at all. It was exactly the same. Koji was brought up listening to records every day. It was no strain for him to practice really well. Good practicing is bound to produce fine results; that is why three-year-old Koji played "Humoresque" so well—not because he was a genius.

More and more young students came to our house for lessons, and it was very lively. I took the greatest pleasure and delight in giving lessons to children, and all became my friends.

Before long, the war started. I went to distant Kiso-Fukushima to work in a wood factory. Later I settled in Matsumoto.

My little friends become fine people

Close to thirty years have passed, and all my former student-friends are today fine adults, which fills me with deep, profound joy.

After a lapse of so many years I cannot recollect the names of all the pupils of those old days, but I shall enumerate a few students who come to mind—

Toshiya Eto—Professor at Curtis Institute
Yoko Arimatsu—Member of Brussels Music Academy Orchestra
Takeshi Kobayashi—Concertmaster in Czechoslovakia
Kenji Kobayashi—Member of Juilliard School Orchestra
Koji Toyoda First concertmaster of Berlin Radio Symphony Orchestra.
Hidetaro Suzuki—Concertmaster of Quebec Symphony Orchestra
Nejiko Suwa—Member of Brussels Academy Orchestra

All these pupils (everyone else too) had been admitted to Talent Education entirely without any preliminary tests.

Any child can be trained, and there is but one way

That is my assertion, and that it works is demonstrated by the brilliant achievements of the lively children of those early classes. Toshiya at eleven received the first prize of the Ministry of Education in a newspaper music contest. The requirement was Bach's A-minor concerto. Little Koji, seven years old, could play this music beautifully. I wanted the judging committee to know that even a Japanese scarcely seven years old could reach this level too and pass the test. To make them understand clearly that I wanted them to let Koji play, I told them, "Gentlemen, I beg you to listen to Koji Toyoda playing this concerto. You need not score him."

Koji, at seven, had already been brought up and trained to reach this level.

We leave Tokyo

Alone to the factory in Kiso-Fukushima. . . .

In 1943, I was forty-five years old. That year saw the German army defeated at Stalingrad and the turning point of the war in the Pacific Ocean. The Japanese army was forced to withdraw from Guadalcanal, and life became extremely hard and distressing. My father had converted the violin factory to make seaplane floats. But the supply of essential Japanese cypress wood did not come in; so even though we desperately wanted to work, we could not. Unless someone could go into the Kiso-Fukushima mountains for the cypress and bring it down, our work would come to a halt. I visited my father in Nagoya to tell him about the situation and to find out how to get permission to enter the forest.

As long as I stayed in Tokyo, most of my young students refused to be evacuated. Yet the air raids seemed to be getting worse, and the feeling was that it was the time to leave Tokyo. I was instructor at the Imperial Music School as well as at the Kunitachi Music

School, and told the authorities there my plans. The judges of the committee for contests of the Mainichi newspaper had also turned in their resignation.

As the bombing became more and more intense, my wife urged me to leave Tokyo and move to Hakone, where we had a small cottage near Lake Ashi that we used for fishing. She refused to leave me and go away alone, so I finally agreed to evacuate too. Circumstances, however, prevented us in the end from being evacuated together.

In order to supervise the obtaining of lumber from the forests for our Nagoya factory, it became necessary for me to move to Kiso-Fukushima. But for my wife, who was German, it was not feasible to join me there, in spite of her having lost her German citizenship when she married me and being, then, a Japanese subject by marriage. Nor did it matter that Germany was an ally of Japan. All foreigners were looked upon with suspicion, and life was made extremely difficult and unpleasant for them. During the war, the Germans in Japan were evacuated to the mountain resorts of Karuizawa and Hakone, and since we had a cottage at Hakone, the only expedience was for my wife to go there alone. Food was terribly scarce, but at Hakone she would at least be able to draw a special German ration (bread instead of rice, and so on). Reluctantly we decided to part for the duration of the war, hoping that it would not be for long.

She had almost no freedom of movement and could not leave the "German village" to come and see me, but I could visit her from time to time. On one such visit I still remember vividly the precious apple she had saved for me from her rations. But I felt it was even too precious for me to enjoy. I also saved it, without telling my wife, for the children in Kiso-Fukushima.

And so it was that I went alone to live among the mountains of Kiso-Fukushima and took over a *geta* (wooden clog) factory there, converting it into a lumberyard to supply our float factory in Nagoya. I knew almost nothing about the factory, but from the forest I was able to get first-class timber, which we sawed and sent off to Nagoya. This we did with remarkable speed.

Work went on smoothly. The manufacture of floats made good progress. I had always made it a rule to live as best I could, whatever

happened, whatever work I had to do, so I was able to throw myself
into the work at hand and gain from it. In my youth, a Zen priest
named Dogen had taught me this. The lumber-mill work was interesting, and we carried on cheerfully.

Eating river moss to ward off starvation

The war, however, became worse and worse. Even the distribution of provisions came to a standstill. Kiso-Fukushima is a town
in a valley on the upper reaches of the river Kiso. Surrounded as
it is by mountains and small valleys, no food is produced. Close to
the last stages of the war there was no more distribution of rations,
but because ours was a war factory, there was a possibility of obtaining things on the black market. However, I positively did not
want to buy on the black market. At that time, my younger sister,
who had lost her husband, came with her two children to live with
me.

On factory holidays we all went into the heart of the mountains
to look for *warabi* (bracken), but often there was nothing left to
eat; other people had already picked it all. We then went along the
mountain stream and found some water algae on a rock. It had a
tinge of redness and a stalk. We stuffed our rucksacks to the brim
with this and carried it home. We put it in a big pot with water,
added a little salt, and let it boil. The pot seemed to overflow with
the stuff, but after boiling there remained only half a rice bowl full.
This, unlike mere drinking water, gave us some feeling that we had
eaten gruel. In this manner we frequently kept off hunger. It must
have been bitter for my sister, not being able to feed her children.
But I will remember the kindness and goodness of the people in the
Fukushima locality all my life.

We stayed in a house with a family named Doke, which included
an old man. They all helped us warmheartedly. If they managed to
get some good things to eat, we always were called; after such a treat
the household would come to life again.

"Koji, I am in Kiso-Fukushima. . ."

The war became harsher and crueler. Yet there were no air raids in Kiso-Fukushima, the small town in the mountains. I felt responsible for the factory workers; and since I could do nothing else, I played the violin for them every morning in the clear mountain air. Meals and living conditions were miserable. At the factory we all joined together and worked desperately hard every day.

Then the war ended.

At about that time we happened to hear that both of Koji's parents had died, one after the other. Hurriedly I sent a letter of inquiry to their old address in Tokyo. Of course, there was no answer. Then I asked a friend in Tokyo where Koji Toyoda and his younger brother would most likely have moved. Koji's father had moved to Tokyo because of me; what had become of the two very young boys now that both parents were gone? This I could not neglect. I asked the NHK (Nippon Broadcasting Station) to broadcast a message on their missing-persons program: "Koji Toyoda, I am in Kiso-Fukushima. Please let me know where you are." About two months later a letter arrived from a man named Toyoda. It was Koji's uncle; he had taken care of him.

Koji becomes a member of our family

"We found Koji."

"How lucky, how lucky, indeed!"

"Let's ask him to come here."

"Let's write him at once. . . ."

I was filled with joy. Soon afterward, Koji, now eleven, came with his uncle to Kiso-Fukushima. He had grown, for it was three years since we had last seen him. My sister and her children were also glad when Koji came to live with us. In Hamamatsu the uncle ran a small *sake* (Japanese rice wine) drinking place. "Far from playing violin, he helped me daily in the shop," the uncle said. He begged me to take care of Koji, then went home. From that day, Koji

became a member of our family. And when he was nineteen, I sent
him to study abroad. My sister gave him a great deal of motherly
love and brought him up together with her own children. Koji enjoyed life in Kiso-Fukushima.

Our family now consisted of seven people. There were my aunt
with her girl helper, three children, my sister, and I. Every night we
did something pleasant, such as each making up a haiku (Japanese
poem) and reading it. The poetry wasn't very good, but the pastime
was amusing, even hilarious.

We all did our best for the benefit of Koji

The three years Koji had spent helping his uncle in the environment of the sake bar had entirely altered his Tokyo form of education. We noticed in him an undesirable behavior and attitude. We
began scolding and grumbling. What was there to do? But scolding
does no good and should be avoided.

One day, while Koji was away at school, I told my sister, "For
the last three years, Koji has not been aware of his coarse manners
or his habit of leaving things in disorder or half done. But we all
know that by scolding he will certainly fancy himself wronged and
grow up with this kind of feeling. There has to be a better way."
Yasuo and Mitsuo, my sister's children, were told too that the whole
household would do no more grumbling but that we all would have
to display better manners and conduct in our daily life. "If we create
such an environment, Koji will, without noticing it, become a good
child, and his life will not be harmfully distorted by scolding."

I made this proposal to my aunt, my sister, and the girl helper,
andthey agreed. The next day, we silently directed our daily life
toward achieving a better attitude and good manners. For Koji's sake
we all worked together and were mutually inspired. It was for Koji's sake, but it turned out to be for the sake of all of us, and good
for our minds and conduct.

Two years passed. In the meantime Koji melted into our way of
life. The bruises of three years left no traces, and he became a well
brought up child.

The Talent Education movement begins

The Talent Education movement started in 1945. It was the end of our three years' life in Kiso-Fukushima. In Matsumoto, among the culture-minded, there was talk of founding a music school. By chance, Mrs. Tamiki Mori, a singer who had taught with me at the Imperial Music School, had been evacuated to Matsumoto. She was interested in the proposed school, and she sent a message to me in Kiso-Fukushima, asking me to come to Matsumoto and help.

I sent the following answer: "I am not very interested in doing 'repair' work on people who can play already. I did enough of that before in Tokyo. What I want to try is infant education. I have worked out a new method I want to teach to small children—not to turn out geniuses but through violin playing to extend the child's ability. I have been doing this research for many years. That is why I want to put all my efforts into this kind of education in the future. If my idea finds approval, I will help with teaching along these lines."

After a while the answer came from Matsumoto that they had consented to my terms and wanted help. Thus it was that I came to settle in Matsumoto. At first, I commuted once a week back and forth between the two cities. But before long, I found that wasn't enough. Many people kindly urged me to move to Matsumoto, and we finally did. In this manner our Talent Education movement started at the Matsumoto Music School.

Koji always with God

As I have said, my sister Hina was like a mother to Koji and looked after him well. In Matsumoto, Koji made the acquaintance of a Catholic priest and went to church every Sunday. Before long he became a devout Catholic. My sister, close in heart to Koji, accompanied him to church on Sundays, and half a year later she became a Catholic too. She helped with work for the church, as well as helping me with my Talent Education movement. Later, though still a young boy, Koji went to the Paris Conservatory to study.

I had the following discussion with my sister: "Eventually Koji may want to take up studies to become a priest."

"Yes, it is possible. For Koji, art and religion are the same."

"I was sure he would become a musician, but if by any chance he wants to enter a theological school it is all right; we will not hinder him."

Koji became an excellent musician. But we had had this conversation because of his strong religious feeling.

Koji was then about fourteen. His violin tone was beautiful and admirable, his musical sense high. He had reached the point where he could give a fine performance. One day the following incident happened.

Association with fine people helps develop nobility and beauty of character

After a lesson, I said to Koji, who played Bach's Chaconne very well, "Today you should go to church and play there before Christ. If you play with all your heart and soul, He will listen."

"Yes, I will go," said Koji, and he took his violin and went to church, just around the corner.

After an hour he came back. "I played the Chaconne in church."

"Good. How was it?"

"There was no one present; I felt very good."

"That's fine. Wherever and whenever you play, always think that Christ is listening to you. All right?"

Koji's cheerful face became even brighter as he answered yes. Gentle, obedient Koji!

I think it is important for their personality development that young people come in contact with distinguished persons. From my experience, I strongly feel that they absorb something of the heart, feeling, and deeds of such persons. Because of this belief I selected teachers for Koji—Mitsuhiko Sekiya and his wifed—whom I esteemed. Mr. Sekiya is now a professor at International Christian

University, and formerly taught at Shinshu University in Matsumoto. I begged Mr. Sekiya to take Koji into his family and Mrs. Ayako Sekiya, his wife, to teach him English, so that Koji would be able to pass the test for going abroad to France to study. At the same time I hoped Mr. Sekiya would be kind enough to teach him French. For Koji to have been with this couple of wonderful characters for such a length of time is the most wonderful thing that could have happened to him. I too am grateful.

A test of training

In another part of this book I asked, "What is talent, ability?" I reiterate, it does not exist at birth but has to be created. Here, in connection with Koji Toyoda, I want to relate the following incident. Koji, and Kenji (Kobayashi)—we called them Ko-chan and Ken-chan—were very good friends. Both were about fifteen years of age. Kenji lived in Tokyo. As soon as his school lessons were over, he took his violin and came to Matsumoto for recreation during vacations. What fun it was to idle the time away! One day a request came from the Matsumoto NHK broadcasting station for a radio performance. I thought this a good opportunity, and wanted them to play the Vivaldi concerto for two violins. They had never played it before. I decided to test the two boys to see how much they could remember. I gave the broadcasting station the name of the music, but did not tell Koji and Kenji until the morning of the preceding day. I called them from their room and gave them the music, telling them, "This music has to be played tomorrow at 1:00 P.M. at a radio broadcast. It is rather sudden, but it will be a good exercise for you. You'd better start practicing right away." Both were surprised, saying, "This is awful," and so on, but they took their respective music books and ran joyfully to their room. In a few moments I heard the tune of the concerto for two violins. When, after an hour and a half, I thought I would call their attention to certain points in the musical expression and went upstairs to their room, both of them played the first movement without looking at the notes. It was simply amazing.

Off to the broadcasting station without any music

I left the two practicing, and went on an errand. When we all met at suppertime, I said, "Well, can you manage?"

"Well, sir, you certainly startled us today. It's lovely music, isn't it?"

Although they accused me of pulling a fast one on them, they seemed to enjoy it and there was no sign of anxiety or uneasiness. Before they went to the broadcasting station the next day, I wanted to hear their performance. Both handed over their music books, which I took and put on the table, and then I listened to their playing. (It has always been our custom for the children to give the music books to the teacher before playing.) After the two had finished, I said, "You played very well. Your tone and musical intepretation are indeed fine. Now, play there just as well. I will listen here." They went out to the waiting car in high spirits. They had left the music books, of course, on the table.

As I point out at another place in this book, I put great store on memory training. My students must know the music by heart and not refer to written notes. Both these boys have been taught like this from childhood; it didn't even occur to them to take the music along.

The time comes to secure the best teacher for Koji

Ability grows as it is trained. . . .

After the two had left, I reflected again on this: "It was only yesterday that I gave them the concerto. They did not know it, yet they played all movements today thoroughly memorized and with no sense of insecurity or apprehension." My test was completed.

The broadcast was indeed a beautiful performance. All the family listened together, and we were filled with joyous emotion. Now those two are fine musicians. I wonder whether they still think of this episode.

Naturally, both had been accepted at Talent Education without any test, and then were trained. As I said before, I don't consider great talent to be a possibility for exceptional persons only. *Everyone* brought up in this manner is trained to show talent and has the potential for it. Koji and Kenji are simply two examples.

Koji, a member of our family, turned nineteen. The time had come to select the best teacher for him and for his art. The one we selected was the Rumanian Georges Enesco (1881-1955), one of the twentieth century's finest artists and most distinguished violinists.

"I am speechless"

Enesco was already at a considerable age, but I knew that he was still in Paris. I wanted Koji to go to Paris and study under this fine personality and supreme artist. In November, 1952, three years before Enesco died, I received a letter from Koji with the following news: "I passed the Paris Conservatory entry examination. Professor Benedetti is now my teacher. From a friend I heard that Professor Enesco is ill, and does not take on students."

"I am speechless," I wrote by return mail. "I really don't know what to say. Didn't I want you to go abroad to study in Paris under Enesco? To hear from a friend that Professor Enesco is ill and not to see for yourself, what kind of thing is that? You left Japan because I wanted you to study with this teacher. If you hold the teacher in high regard, then you will not just listen to hearsay but will investigate yourself, aside from the question of whether or not you will receive lessons. That is an entirely different matter."

After a while a happy letter from Koji arrived. It had the following touching message: "I received your letter and I think I really matured reading it. I looked up Professor Enesco's address and at once went to see him. I did meet him. He is a great, wonderful person. Advanced in years, and despite the fact that he felt a little weak he said, 'Go ahead and play.' Professor Enesco was so kind as to listen to me play the Chaconne by Bach. After I finished, the maestro said, 'It is fine if you study with me here. But now you are a pupil of Benedetti and I cannot be so impolite as to take his student away. When you have graduated from the Paris Conservatory, you will be welcome.' Professor, I will make every possible effort to graduate as quickly as I can."

I sent Koji this answer: "Dear Koji: Thank you for your letter. . . . Wasn't it good that you visited Professor Enesco? You will one day realize that it is the greatest and best blessing on earth to come in contact with men of high humanism, who also through their art have a pure, noble soul. And whatever you can absorb of his greatness and beauty of character will determine your worth as a person. However, to perceive and grasp these qualities requires the humility and judgment that come only through sincerity, love, and knowledge. That you can be close to Professor Enesco makes me, above all, feel at ease, confident, and happy. It is greedy of me, but I would like one more person close to you: Dr. Schweitzer. This really would be most wonderful. But however wonderful the other person may be, it depends on us alone—whether we have the capacity to absorb their greatness. One has to educate oneself from within to benefit from the greatness of others. Only if one can do this can one fully realize the joy of being near someone who is great. Never lose your humility, for pride obscures the power to perceive truth and greatness. Please, by all means, don't forget this."

Koji graduates from the Paris Conservatory in half a year

Half a year later there were graduation examinations at the Paris Conservatory. Koji graduated from the conservatory in the surprising time of a mere six months. Anybody would take great pleasure in graduating from such a famous school; in Koji's case it was not so much the joy of receiving a diploma as being able to become a pupil of Professor Enesco, after that first meeting a half year before. During the following two years, until this great master passed away, he taught Koji. How many noble and valuable things Koji learned can only be imagined.

Koji had grown to be a young man when he lost Professor Enesco, and he therefore was able to single out a teacher for himself. His choice was Arthur Grumiaux, a teacher at the Royal Music School in Brussels, who also gave concerts and recitals, made record-dings and was perhaps the most distinguished violinist in Europe at that time. When Koji heard Grumiaux play at a concert, he decided that he wanted him as a teacher.

Koji became Grumiaux's number one pupil. There were two persons this teacher was most attached to, and both are Japanese. Both studied with me from infancy. One, needless to say, was Koji Toyoda; the other, who also became Grumiaux's pupil, was Tomiko Shida, who won top prize at the International Music Contest in Munich in 1963.

In 1964, when Grumiaux and his wife came to Japan at the invitation of the Osaka International Festival, he came to Matsumoto and there I saw and met for the first time my former pupils' foreign teacher. His concert was wonderfully artistic.

To come in contact with such a personality is fortunate—a good, warmhearted person with noble spirit, human kindness, simplicity, and naturalness. For Koji and Tomiko, I was very happy, and I felt secure in knowing them to be under good tutelage. Tomiko Shida played beautifully before she went abroad, and I was glad that she found a teacher who would polish her ability even more.

To attain high art and musical sense a pure mind is absolutely indispensable. About 1960, the following happened with Tomiko Shida.

Just play for the spirit of Chausson

For the Talent Education summer school about a thousand people—pupils and their mothers—come from all districts of Japan to Matsumoto. Every night concerts are held.

Before going to Europe, Tomiko was scheduled to play "Poème" by Chausson (1865–1899). Shortly before the performance she told me, "Professor, it is so difficult I am afraid."

I said, "What are you afraid of? You don't play this beautiful piece for the audience. You are not showing off your ability to them. Stop thoughts like that. If you make a mistake, just go over the passage again. Tonight you play for the spirit of Chausson. This wonderful poetry, heart, inspiration—play it together with your own,

then there is nothing to be afraid of. Just think, besides Chausson
and you, there is nobody in the world."

That night she really played wonderfully. I was moved to tears
when I went up to the stage to shake her hand. Later she became
a proud pupil of Grumiaux's.

To lament lack of talent is folly

I spent most of my twenties abroad studying in Berlin. Arriving
in Germany, I looked for the best violin teacher and found him in
Professor Karl Klingler. The professor gave me some difficult music
as homework. I practiced every day for five hours, but however hard
I tried, it was as if a big wall prevented my advance. This continued
many days, many months. I didn't get ahead at all. A sad resignation settled over me. "It is hopeless, I have no talent."

Besides, I heard concerts of great musicians that only discouraged
me more. To hear the famous Berlin Philharmonic Orchestra, filled
with so many excellent players, affected me adversely and made me
even more miserable and helpless. "What a pity! Without talent, trying so hard, every day—it's not worth it," I told myself. I felt that
I had no ability, and wanted to die. This kind of feeling more or
less afflicts every young person, especially those who want to em-
brace art closely. Seeing the great work and talent of predecessors
and comparing it with his or her own ability, as well as being told
that talent is inborn, can make a young person melancholy and filled
with despair.

However little talent one thinks he/she has, one should at least try

Many young people who doubt their talent may even entertain
suicidal thoughts. But instead of being morose, without hope, they
should begin by saying, "Talent is *not* inborn, it has to be created."
If one knows this, he or she can be buoyed up with hope even though
the road is one of hardship and distress. Exertion is always beneficial
as long as one is aware that it is goal oriented.

From the time I left Japan it was not my objective to become a performer. Fascinated by music, I wanted to learn the secret of this man-made art. What is art? I wanted to know. Despairing and disillusioned by my lack of performing ability, I was spurred on by hurt pride in my quest for the secret of art. And it cured my despair. Even if I had no talent, and even if my progress was slow, I determined to plod on step by step toward my goal of becoming a whole, well-rounded human being. I did not hurry, but I did not rest either. I endeavored ceaselessly. And it gave me both peace of mind and something to live for.

I learn the foolishness of lamenting lack of talent

My devotion to art helped me to develop and educate my own ability. "I have no talents—what sadness and despair are occasioned by this nonsensical belief! For years, people everywhere have succumbed to this false way of thinking, which is really only an excuse for avoiding work. After long studies over a period of time, I finally learned that man is the product of his environment. Had I known earlier that ability can be developed by training, I would have followed the right path much earlier.

Every child can be educated; it is only a matter of the method of education. Anyone can train himself; it is only a question of using the right kind of effort.

To surrender to the thought of having no talent and give up the effort is cowardly

Poor training produces poor ability. People should make every effort, even though it is difficult, to accumulate and build superior ability. This I want to impress on your minds.

Well, then, what is the right and correct effort? I will discuss this later. Here I only want you to remember one thing—repetition. After one has learned a thing, it should be thoroughly mastered by repeating it again and again.

Science does not pretend to explain what it does not understand. So people who know anything at all about science should not voice opinions, such as "inborn talent," with regard to human ability. What does science really know about human potential at birth? Superstitions about talent training should be discarded. To reason whether one has talent or not is to no avail. Abandon these thoughts, and use your own power to create talent.

Look at the facts: Clumsiness is a result of wrong training

While I was teaching at the Imperial Music School, one of the girl students told me, "Professor, I am so clumsy, and my fingers won't move quickly."

"Clumsy? Who decided that?" I asked. Then followed this dialogue.

"I think so."

"Then you misjudged yourself. You make a mistake in calling yourself clumsy. It's the same as if you applied the brake on a car and then complained that it wouldn't run properly."

"But my fingers don't move fast enough."

"Did you hurt them or have an injury?"

"No."

"Just put your left hand on the table. All right. Now try together with me to move the first finger, as if we were playing piano. Whose finger moves faster?. . . There, didn't it move fast? You see, there's nothing wrong with your fingers. Your head and fingers are not working together, that's all. If they don't work in cooperation, your practice is no good. One can say that your manner of practicing has been very poor indeed."

"What can I do?"

"When I was your age, I also practiced vigorously in a mistaken, wrong manner. There was no one to tell me. Now, try this: from today on, place your fingers slowly and carefully in the positions you want to reach fast. Repeat over and over again for three days. On the fourth day do it a little faster and continue for two more days. On the sixth day you should be able to do it fast without difficulty."

She practiced in the way I advised, and at the next lesson her fingers moved with speed and accuracy and there was no complaint.

The joy of thirty workers

I was invited to a large factory to give an address to the workers. After the lecture, the director, following some pleasantries, said, "Our factory employs about thirty manual workers. Even though they try their best, work is proceeding very slowly. It seems they are born that way. Is there something Talent Education can do about it? We're in the red."

I was thinking of the girl student with the slow-moving fingers. "You say their hands are slow. It is not their hands but their heads that are slow."

"Not the hands?"

I told the director to hire a good coach and let the workers play table tennis every day for an hour during working hours. "Then head and body have to work together, and I'm sure it will improve their efficiency in their working habits."

"This is an interesting proposal," the director said. He tried it, and about half a year later I received a glowing letter: "Thanks to you the workers' efficiency has unbelievably improved, just as you said. I am so very happy. Besides working so well now, they have table tennis for their recreation. I would like very much to show you how your advice worked."

Hiroko-Chan—extra slow in everything

I started to learn violin playing when I was seventeen. My little finger was utterly imcompetent, for, of course, during the previous seventeen years it had not been trained to play the violin. I wanted it to move efficiently, but it wouldn't. In the case of the trill there was no expression and my incompetence was apparent. I wanted my little finger to at least come close to the ability of the other fingers, and I practiced daily for many years. But even now, after more than

forty years, it still hasn't caught up with the expression and ability
of the other fingers. What is not trained while we are growing, brings
pain and aches later. This becomes even clearer to me when I teach
four- and five-year-old children. Their little fingers are trained from
the beginning with the other fingers, and I envy them when I see
how easily and skillfully those tiny fingers can be trained. Sense, feeling and ability, too, can be easily educated with time and practice.

Hiroko was a girl of six. Brought up in a remote part of Manchuria, she was repatriated after the war. Her grandmother heard
one of my lectures and brought her to the Matsumoto Music School.
This Hiroko, educated in the wilds of Manchuria, was indeed more
than slow in all her movements. Whatever she did was slow and could
stand no comparison with what other children did. I was anxious
about it and tried this tactic:

On the second floor of the school I lined up Hiroko with children
of her age group and gave everyone a number. Then, standing in
front of them, I called out, "Attention, everybody. When I call one,
two, three, put your right hand on top of your head as fast as you
can—at the word three, remember, not before or after." This training ability is necessary for fine violin playing. Children enjoy this
game very much. Before a rehearsal I let them play it to loosen them
up, and, without fail, they are besides themselves with pleasure,
laughing and giggling. But Hiroko alone was very slow in putting
her hand on her head. She really took her time, as if time were nonex-
istent. More than playing violin, I wanted her to change her pace
of movement. I continued the game with all the children. Finally
Hiroko could play violin well, and did her best to move with alacrity.
The next twelve or thirteen years showed a surprising change. She
became alert and active, and she acquired a large repertoire of music.
Now Hiroko Yamada is the only Japanese girl member of the Berlin
Radio Orchestra.

Ten years' effort can change inferiority into superior talent

Shortcomings or weak points in children are usually blamed on
"character" or "nature" and are left at that. But through training,

the contrary—points of excellence—can be brought out in a ten-year program. If he or she really goes about it in earnest, anyone can cultivate ability in ten years, I believe. Even in one year, shortcomings can be changed into good points if only we set our aims high enough. Continuing for ten years, we can become outstanding indeed. Thus in our own life, we can show great vitality if training is properly carried out.

Everyone has shortcomings. The most common one is the tendency to say "I will do this, or that" and then not to do it right away. This habit of procrastination will influence a person's fate throughout life. Developing ability depends on action and the directing of our attention to doing things.

By repeating an action for only three days or so, nothing whatsoever will happen—certainly not success. That's why only to think that "I want to do this" and not to acquire the habit of doing it continuously accomplishes nothing much.

There is no limit to our shortcomings. Until we die, we should spare no time or effort in changing our weaknesses to merits. To do so can be pleasant and interesting. We can become like the horse that starts last and yet outruns the field, reaching the wire first; it is the same fun.

The high-jumping ability of the Ninjutsu—a lesson to be learned

I want to talk a little more about cultivating one's ability.

A book I once read told how the Ninjutsu were taught to high-jump: "Take a hemp seed and cultivate it, and every day leap over the plant" was one of the methods. The way to produce superior ability is to concentrate on something and devote oneself to doing it.

Hemp grows fast. To a person watching it daily it doesn't seem so, but the growth of the hemp goes on hourly without recess. By leaping over the hemp every day one's leaping ability grows together with the hemp. After a month or two of one's having not seen it for some time, the hemp will suddenly seem to have grown to a surprising height. If in the meantime one's jumping ability has not been trained, and suddenly one wants to jump over the hemp, it will prove

to be impossible. But if one has worked hard together with the growing hemp, it will seem natural to leap over it easily.

The reason that we chatter freely in Japanese is that we use it
daily; it is the same with jumping over the hemp every day from
the time it appears. It is a matter of "Ease comes with training."
We simply have to train and educate our ability, that is to say, do
the thing over and over again until it feels natural, simple, and easy.

That is the secret.

Look at your right hand

Ability does not just come about without training. We have to
educate it in ourselves. Everyone has to train his own self. Stop
lamenting lack of talent and develop talent instead.

For righthanded people, the left hand is inferior to the right hand.
That is only because the left hand has been relatively idle. The two
hands would be the same if we habitually trained them equally from
the beginning; otherwise they will seem different. It is the same with
human ability. Not to try to educate your talent, thinking that by
nature or birth you don't have any, is your own folly. If you trained
yourself every day to do a specific act, your energy would develop,
your senses would become educated, your ability would expand. Look
at your right hand. Your right hand excels over your left hand
because you yourself brought this about. At birth your left hand was
not inferior; the hands were evenly matched—and see how they have
changed! Similarly, whatever ability we have we were not born with
but have developed ourselves through training. Ability is something
we produce ourselves.

Your right hand knows this. Why has your right hand its extraordinary ability? Repetition. People too can develop superior talent
through the same method—repetition. To stop training as soon as
one can do something does not mean that it is truly absorbed. One
must continue to practice until it is natural and easy. The more one
practices, the better one becomes. Talent is born this way. Far from
being inferior to the right hand, the left hand would display the same
ability if we kept using it in the same way.

The beauty of earnest repetition

Expend effort on improving yourself. To think that you are born with an ability that develops by itself is a mistake. If some skill is easy for you, that is evidence that it has been developed through training to such an extent that it has become a part of you. "Become a part of you" is to say that your purpose has been achieved by work and repetition until the skill has firmly taken hold in your consciousness.

I learned that through self-discipline during my studying in Germany when, longing to do better and reach self-awakening, I had to face my own inability to perform. I think that to realize this is very important, not only for the young but also for older people. Now, too, I always try not to forget this. For instance, I recently wrote, "Tone has a living soul without form" on 1,500 *shikishi* (squares or oblongs of cardboard covered with silk), used for writing Japanese *waka* poems. I presented one to each little graduate at the annual March concert. Many people say this is a terrible task. I have to get up very early every morning to be able to do it besides my other work, but far from finding it terrible, I enjoy it, and want to write especially nice. I rub the *sumi* (China-ink stick) and write those words on every single leaf. Not a calligrapher, I nevertheless try to improve my writing with every shikishi, and self-confidence is added with each one. I work with vigor, and it becomes, although only in my way, splendid calligraphy. Yet one sheet is not like another. I cannot tell how much satisfaction I get out of this work and how wonderful the repetition feels.

Develop excellence through repetition

My self-discipline has become, in other words, the Talent Education method. My own wrong training efforts of the past have been discarded. In their place is a correct and sound method. In most cases, if one is able to play a piece of music, there will follow in rapid succession other pieces—this one, that one too, and many

others. But just "playing through" many pieces is not good training if there will be no one piece that is really played excellently. Just
being able to say "I can play all these pieces" is in fact insufficient,
for it results in not developing musical sense, fine interpretation and
so on.

This principle applies not only to music but to all other faculties.
It is fundamental to develop the planted ability to the highest possible point. Learn one thing, then practice and polish it every day for
perhaps three months. If you are learning to play an instrument during this time, listen continuously to the best performers in the world
on records. Soon you will improve, playing more and more
excellently, until a new, higher level is born. By this time it is no
longer technique only but the possession of spirit and heart.

While playing violin, finishing a phrase is the spiritual attitude
in music; it is an important matter of time. Although the piece has
ended, the music has not (for a certin instant). Bach, for instance,
used to write *Fermate* in ink into his music textbooks of the eigh-
teenth century. The tranquility during prayers, dropping silently to
one's knees, is like this important moment. A man who has reached
this grade will attain a noble heart and mind in addition to artistic
sense, and will rise above and be far ahead of others.

Don't rush, but don't rest; patience is an important faculty for achievement

Ability is one thing we have to produce (or work for) ourselves.
That means to repeat and repeat an action until it becomes a part
of ourselves. It is easy to say, but to have the energy to do it—there
lies the problem. There are many people who resolve they will achieve
this or that, but not all carry out their intentions. They start, perhaps,
but they don't really go on, and they don't put enough strength into
their efforts, leaving things half done. Indeed, isn't this the experience
of many, many people? There are only a few who go through with
their purpose and accomplish things. Whatever work it may be, the
way to success is, after all, to stick to one's intentions to the vey
last. Everyone is able to do it; it depends only on one's will.

Achievement is the product of energy and patience, which have
to be trained like all other abilities. And we have to be brought up

with this idea. How can we work well otherwise? We ourselves have to awaken to this fact. In the beginning, forbearance and patience decide one's fate. Why? If we endure and continue to expend energy to achieve a goal, the necessary patience will develop; thus, our capacity to achieve will grow and grow. This attained ability will help us to work much easier, at the same time building up our energy and perseverance.

Natural growth

If we cannot be patient but stop a project halfway through—then later start again, drop it, start again, and so on—this kind of repetition will not bring good results. A person who works like that will never rise over difficulties; in the end, he or she will give up the effort as entirely useless and utterly hopeless. Many young people's unhappiness is caused by such reasoning. Let's think again of the example of a tree. A seed is planted in the earth. We don't see when the germination begins. That is the doing of Mother Nature; it is the fundamental working principle. We have to wait patiently. We cannot dig up the seed to see whether it is really growing; to do so would be to destroy everything.

Suddenly a bud appears. What a joy and pleasure to watch it grow! At the same time the root, unseen in the ground, is getting stronger and has the power to produce a big, sturdy tree. I think this is a good analogy for one's ability. Once the "seed" ability is planted, it has to be carefully and patiently tended. Finally the "bud," or talent, presents itself and has to be educated and brought up with perseverance until the "root," or power, becomes very strong and is indissolubly tied to the personality. It can be said to be a treasure when a person can accomplish and carry through his or her work to the very last.

Without hurry, without rest

To make a resolution and act accordingly is to live with hope. Confronted with a high mountain, you cannot reach the summit in

one stride, but must climb step by step to approach your goal. There
may be difficulties and hardships, but not disappointment or despair
if you follow the path steadily. Do not hurry. This is a fundamental
rule. If you hurry and collapse or tumble down, nothing is achieved.
Do not rest in your efforts; this is another fundamental rule. Without
stopping, without haste, carefully taking a step at a time forward
will surely get you there. To commit yourself to untiring patience
and strong endurance, what we call *kan*—intuition or sixth sense—
is an absolute necessity in education. Without it, Dr. Hakushi
Yukawa wouldn't have discovered his mesotron theory. At least, so
I believe.

A dot of light for a child living in darkness

One morning Mr. Tanaka, a painter in oils, visited me with a
letter of introduction from a friend of mine. He was leading a little
boy by the hand. The boy was blind. Mr. Tanaka said, "This is my
son, Teiichi, five years old. As a baby he suffered from an eye
disease, and since it was a matter of life or death, he had to be
operated on and both eyes had to be extracted. My wife and I want
to give our son a light in his darkness, a light that will shine
throughout his life. We were thinking of music, and I came to ask
you to accept him as one of your violin students."

Looking at the innocent little boy who throughout his life would
have to find his way around, feeling and groping with his hands,
I couldn't help the tears welling up in my eyes. I could not
immediately say all right, but had to figure out a way to coach a
totally blind child.

"Please wait one week," I answered. "If I think I will be able
to do it, and have enough self-confidence to teach this youngster,
then I will see to it that it turns out to be a success."

That night in my quiet study room I thought about the difficult
problem. How could I teach this blind child? I had no idea. After
a while it suddenly occurred to me that first of all I should be in
the same condition as a blind person. I rose from my chair and ex-

tinguished the light. In pitch darkness I sat down again. "Well, this is it. I have to find out what it is like to be in complete darkness; then I will understand better the dark world of the blind." The room seemed to be a vacant space. I could not see my violin or bow (yet I knew they were right there). The four strings . . . their positions . . . just a little rising and falling to carry the bow over the other strings . . . the difficulty of violin playing—how to make the boy comprehend all that? In the complete darkness I felt my way around and took violin and bow out of the case and began to play. Apparently for me it is quite the same whether it is bright or dark, since I often play with my eyes closed. I was absolutely conscious of the tip of the bow, the strings, the bridge, the positions. I could "see" it all. I often closed my eyes while playing without particularly thinking about it. But now it dawned on me that we sometimes don't rely on our eyes. By means of *kan* we receive the power of sensibility to play.

Through repeated practice we acquire remarkable strength. Our life activity involuntarily works up a great power, namely the ability of *kan*, that enables us to overcome all difficulties. That's why in this dark world (room) where I could not see anything left or right, I was still able to play. And then. . .

My spiritual eyes open; the promised week passes

"You, I will make little Teiichi see the violin, strings, and bow. He doesn't need physical eyes if I can teach him to use his spiritual ones," I told myself. My basic guiding principle was thus decided. Later I could think about the method. Again Mr. and Mrs. Tanaka showed up with Teiichi. I said, "Let's cooperate and unite all our effort to open the spiritual eyes of the little boy." I asked the parents to be prepared for long, strenuous endeavors and the devotion to carry through the resolution to the very last. Thus lessons began. Even considering that it was for their own child's happiness, Mr. and Mrs. Tanaka cooperated admirably. The anxieties and hardships cannot be put into words, but their dearest wish came true; they put a dot of light in the heart of their son.

The child could see neither up
nor down, right nor left

The first training consisted in making the boy see the bow. "This is called a bow." I put the bow in the little hand, and let him feel from the frog of the bow to the tip, again and agin, so that he was able to remember what a bow is like. Then I taught him how to hold the bow. "Try to move the bow up and down." But his hand moved the bow obliquely. "Next, from right to left." Again there was the slanting movement. His spiritual eyes didn't yet see up or down, right or left. . . . All his movements were equally oblique. "This is your homework for this week, to move the bow up and down, right and left." Of course, I doubted whether he would be able to do it in one week. But I thought that for him to hold the bow and move it as a game, and make the bow at the same time "visible," would correspond with homework, which the parents could easily supervise. After a week he could do this exercise quite well, but still with a curve. The next aim and work was to produce the motion in a straight line, and gradually his homework increased.

The little mouth says, "Yes, I see"

"This time we will try to grasp the tip of the bow with the left hand. Here, take the bow in your right hand—you can see it, can't you?"

"Yes," he replied.

"Then go ahead and grasp the tip way on top of the bow. Don't feel your way up. Let's see whether you can do it in one swift movement. Now seize it—"

Teiichi was interested and enjoying it. But his left hand went way off. In his own playful way he tried it many, many times. There was failure as well as the bow's being sometimes just within his reach.

Mr. and Mrs. Tanaka gazed and stared, as in silent prayer. Then, finally, Teiichi was able to get hold of the bow tip with his left hand. "Good. . . . Now do it five times without a single miss. This will be your homework until the next lesson."

For the blind child a very interesting hobby started. Despite continuous work, only four attempts out of five were successful. Even with only one miss, he had to do it over from the beginning. But while repeating it so often, Teiichi could be confident of his progress. To the question, "You can see the tip of the bow, can't you?" the answer was always, "Yes, I see it." To say "see" is in fact what? Sometimes tears welled in my eyes when Teiichi's little mouth casually gave this answer—he, who didn't know or see the world with his eyes.

Teiichi's daily practice consisted only in getting hold of the bow at a certain point. To know, or "see," the bow and tip with *kan*— this posed the most difficult and important problem.

Then followed the exercise of holding the bow horizontally in front of him and trying to touch the palm of his outstretched left hand with the bow tip. When I play in darkness, I can clearly feel how and where the tip of the bow moves. Teiichi had to acquire the same feeling. The foremost and greatest difficulty for him to overcome was to hold the bow horizontally. When he was able to do that, intuition would take over, I believed.

To touch the palm of the left hand with the tip of the bow is difficult for a blind child. But Teiichi found this to be a splendid new game, and with the help of the family he worked patiently. During his lesson when he hit it off three times in a row and at the fourth time the bow tip would just drift in space, he would sigh, "Oh, dear." But I would encourage him, saying cheerfully, "Well, that was a miss. Let's start all over again, and now you will make it five times continuously." There is no other way to teach *kan*, or any other ability, than through good, energetic practice. In the course of time Teiichi could do this exercise five and six times without failure. Afterward I assigned the following homework: raise the thumb from the outstretched left hand and touch it with the tip of the bow. I thought, "If he can do that, he will really have become a person who sees."

After one severe year—success

We may well imagine how grave it was at first from what Mr. Tanaka said: "This is really not easy to do, but *very* difficult." That was the first week. In the second week the boy was able to do it twice or three times out of five without failure. "Now the Professor too will try once." I thought I would have no trouble at all in doing it. I stared hard at the bow tip, then lifted my left hand, thumb up, aiming the tip of the bow to touch this small point; but it turned aside and missed. Once again a failure. When I finally succeeded, my heart was filled with sympathy for the little blind child, who after two weeks' daily training could do what I had failed to do with open eyes. How often must he have repeated the exercise! But the parents' and child's energy and patience won, and *kan* had been beautifully trained.

After the bow and tip became thus visible, violin practice began. Teiichi's strenuous efforts were rewarded with success, and after one year he could play various pieces just like other children.

When all my young little students—Yoko Arimatsu, Koji Toyoda, Takeshi Kobayashi, Kenji Kobayashi, and so on—gave a concert in Tokyo at Hibiya Hall, six-year-old Teiichi played the Seitz concerto. Watching the blind youngster performing on stage, many people wept.

Kan produces *kan.*

Fated meeting with Prince Yoshichika Tokugawa

Here follows a little episode of self-praise and *kan.*

My father, the proprietor of the Suzuki Violin Factory, sent me to a commercial school because he wanted me to work in his factory in the future. During summer vacations I always worked there, and I got a general idea of violin production. After my graduation I entered the factory as a regular staff member in charge of the export section, packing and booking. I was very busy but happily engaged in this way. When, after two years, I would raise a slight fever every evening, the doctor bade me rest. In late autumn I stayed at an inn at Okitsu for three months to recuperate. There I got acquainted with a fellow lodger, Mr. Yanagida who came from Hokkaido. He was there with his wife and two small children. We soon became friends. Mr. Yanagida told me that he was at one time a schoolmate of Marquis Tokugawa's at the Gakushuin.

After returning to Nagoya, I received an unexpected letter in the early summer from Mr. Yanagida, asking whether I would like to join an expedition for one month to Chishima for biological research, led by Marquis Tokugawa. I could participate in some sightseeing around the islands. The ship was scheduled to sail on the first of August.

When my father agreed to my accepting this invitation, I went to Tokyo to get Marquis Tokugawa's approval of my inclusion. There I met Mr. Tokugawa for the first time, and this encounter decided my entire fate and led me in a new direction. I was then under strong influence of Tolstoy and beginning to have a new outlook on life. And then for forty years Mr. Tokugawa's progressive ideas, philosophy, great personality, and thoughts of truth influenced me. How much effect all this had on my life it is hard to measure.

It was in 1919. The ship—the 1,300-ton *Chifu-Maru*—carried the necessary equipment and material to northern Chishima. The expedition party on board numbered thirty, including Mr. Tokugawa, Mr. Yanagida, members of the Tokugawa Biological Research Institute, and as guests Mrs. Matsudaira, a sister of Mr. Tokugawa; her son; Miss Nobu Koda, a renowned pianist; and me. Miss Koda joined the party because Captain Taii (Gunjii Taii), a brother of hers and the famous writer Rohan Koda, was the first Japanese to set foot on the northern Chishima islands. Intending to be a frontiersman in the northern territory, he had formed an immigrant plan to Shumushu Isle, the northernmost end of Chishima. Miss Koda wanted to visit the place in memory of her brother and his achievements.

Even in August it was chilly in northern Chishima. The sea was an unbelievable, deep blue, and the sky an azure blue conducive to carrying my soul farther away. The seals and a school of whales around Shumushu Bay, the shining beauty of the wildflowers, like a carpet on the lonely island under the sun—this scenery of Chishima made a strong impression on all of us. The friendly contact among the people on board, the happiness and warm feeling, will remain forever in our hearts.

At that time I was inseparable from my violin; it had become a part of me. Since there was a piano in the cabin, I played the violin accompanied by Miss Koda. Young as I was, I didn't think that, after all, Miss Koda was a piano teacher. I now feel rather awkward at recalling this.

Our ship circled the islands and finally arrived at our destination, Shumushu.

While we walked side by side on the beach of Cape Kokutan, the northern end of the island, we discovered a most unusual patch of moss of reddish-cobalt color growing high up a sheer cliff.

"I very badly wish to have some of that moss," said Professor Emoto of the Biological Institute, looking up anxiously.

"I will get it for you from here—it is not necessary to climb up there," I boasted, and borrowed a small scoop from a research member.

In grade school I had been good at throwing stones to catch cicadas, and I once had been pitcher on the baseball team at our commercial school. Hence I had some confidence in myself. They urged me on, but of course thinking it would be impossible. When I looked up at the moss from the point right close to the cliff, it turned out to be situated much higher than expected. "Heavens!" I thought; but there was no turning back now. Gripping the scoop tightly and taking careful aim, I threw the scoop, under the scrutiny of the whole party. "Oh, wonderful, marvelous!" they cried. The scoop, luckily, had plunged right into the moss. It stuck there so firmly, however, that it did not fall down as I expected. Under these circumstances I would lose face and be a failure. Long ago I had thrown a stone at a sparrow perched in a tree, and to my horror it had fallen down, dead. Since then I had forbidden myself ever to throw a stone. But on this occasion I grasped a stone as large as my fist. "Watch out, the scoop will fall down when I hit the handle," I called. Talking nonsense like that, I was filled with anxiety. But strangely enough, the stone did hit the handle of the scoop, which, together with the moss, fell down at our feet, to my great relief. As I listened to their applause, I vowed in my heart never again in my life to do such a foolish thing.

The annual concert

Dr. Suzuki and Koji Toyoda
exchange pleasantries

Dr. Suzuki at a workshop in the States

Pablo Casals hugs Dr. Suzuki
after hearing a performance of
his young pupils in Tokyo

Kan *too has to be trained*

The practice of stone throwing in my childhood thus happened to prove its usefulness at Chishima. To my surprise *kan* worked by itself, spontaneously. Intuition is the reliability slumbering at the base of rational experiences, and it works in an instant when needed. Without training, intuition (just like other abilities) cannot grow. It is a popular but deceptive belief that an individual is born with intuition. If, however, one shows an unexpected display of intuition, or sixth sense, it means that whatever is displayed had been trained before, without being especially noticeable, except in cases of sudden need. To foster intuition—*kan*—there is no other way than training. There is a positive difference in the state of *kan* between a person trained from infancy and another not so trained. While one needs five hundred times of practice, the other needs five thousand times to get the same results. Observing this, people talk about the existence of inborn intuition, and think that some lack skill. We may be misled if we don't go back to the very day of birth to investigate personal history—to consider the origin of present ability. Therefore the most important thing is, as I go back to the former theme, to place one in the best environment from the cradle, to train one in the right ways, and never to forget that a person who fails at five hundred times can succeed at five thousand times.

Kan will grow. I was not an expert in stone throwing by nature. I am now painting in my own way. Indeed, I practiced penmanship for sixty years. To write and paint is not only enjoyable for me but brings pleasure to others, Americans as well as many other people. It has become a resource of my Talent Education Movement, though my pictures are not very skillful. In addition, I am able to describe a performing person's character, his good or bad posture, his handling of the bow, the height of his elbow—everything, just by listening to the sound of his playing. Every year, from December through February, tapes are sent to me from the fourteen or fifteen hundred students of our association. These tapes come from all over the country for the graduation concert. Listening to each one, I record my advice to them, including posture, fingering, bowing movements, and

so on. People wonder how I can "see" all that. It is the result of
thirty years of diligent training, the ability of *kan*.

Illness strikes

Close to the end of 1945, I decided to leave Kiso-Fukushima for
Matsumoto to start Talent Education at the Matsumoto Music
School.

Although the war had finally come to an end, Japan was im-
poverished and everyone's money was frozen. The amount people
were allowed to draw was infinitesimal. When my wife could finally
make her way to Matsumoto to see me, after a grueling nine hours
of standing in a crowded, smoky train, she told me that she had
been extremely fortunate: quite by chance she had been given a job
with the American Red Cross in Yokohama, where the occupation
forces had set up their headquarters. I did not like the idea of her
working or of our continued separation, but under the circumstances
it seemed inevitable.

I had had a weak stomach ever since I was twenty years old, and
my condition at the end of the war was very unsatisfactory. To
recuperate, I rented a room in Asama Spa, a suburb of Matsumoto,
and went to live there by myself. Having to cook for myself was
a bother and nuisance. Very soon I was neglecting my health even
more. Even now, if there is no one to take care of my meals, I don't
eat a bit all day long, but fortunately my wife sees to it that I have
proper nutrition. At that time, because she wasn't able to be with
me, I would simply make a potful of soup, put a rice dumpling (*o-
mochi*) in it to cook, and then eat it. I used what was left over to
put another dumpling in, and just kept on in such a way for three
meals every day, until my health became worse than ever. Finally,
in desperation, I sent for my sister in Kiso-Fukushima.

When my wife found me in this condition on her next visit, she
was very distressed and wanted to give up her job immediately to
be with me, but my sister promised to stay and look after me, and
begged my wife to go on working for the Red Cross, else we would
all starve to death, since Waltraud was the only one earning any
money. Reluctantly she agreed, but she insisted on visiting whenever

possible, although the difficult journey sapped much of her energy and time.

The doctor's diagnosis was not cancer or ulcers but a bad case of atony of the stomach. The violent pain caused by my inactive digestion went together with loss of perception, both physically and mentally.

One day in the cold, frozen Shinshu winter, without knowing what I did, I crawled out of the *Kotatsu* (foot- and hand-warming brazier of charcoal set under a low table covered with a large quilt), went to a corner of the room, leaned my head against the wall, and just groaned. My sister was shocked to see me in this state and quite at a loss what to do. But at least I still had the strength to crawl. After that came a long period of confinement in bed; I couldn't get up at all.

One day Miss Misako Koike, a teacher of piano at the Matsumoto Music School, came to visit me. Completely taken aback at seeing my condition, she hastily summoned Mrs. Uehara, a doctor of Chinese medicine. "This weakness and extreme debility cannot continue," Mrs. Uehara pronounced. "Ten more days and it would have been too late. However, it is only the stomach and intestines; otherwise there is nothing wrong with him. . . . All right, I will begin my treatment right away."

Cured by an excellent herb doctor

Mrs. Uehara, contrary to the instructions of the doctor who wanted me to eat only rice gruel or Western-style soup, prescribed steamed unpolished rice and pickled vegetables. Astonished though I was, I followed and believed in Mrs. Uehara's rough treatment, since I was confronted with death anyway. To my great surprise this diet activated my stomach. A week later I could stand up; within no more than a month, I was able to walk very slowly outside.

So, when I was at death's door, exhausted from mental fatigue, Miss Koike introduced this excellent physician, Mrs. Uehara; I became healthy and energetic, and I am alive today to tell the tale.

Once before when I was convalescing, at Okitsu, I renewed my acquaintance with Marquis Tokugawa, which had resulted in the big change, in my life from a white-collar worker to the world of music. During this second period of convalescence I invented a new system of calculation, not only for multiplication but also for division, addition, and subtraction. I thought, "If I get well again, this will be something I can apply in my Talent Education plan," The Hongo elementary school experimented with my system of arithmetic in the fifties, and it is now part of the curriculum of many elementary schools in Japan, including those in Aichi-Ken, after observation and approval by the Ministry of Education.

One day the principle of Talent Education, based on the way we learn our mother tongue, will certainly change the course of education. No one will be left behind; and based on love, it will foster truth, joy, and beauty as part of a child's character. If nothing else, it will at least teach children during the nine-year compulsory school period to be warmhearted and to enjoy doing kindnesses to others.

In addition to having my life prolonged, many things came out of this second convalescence that can only be called fate.

My father, Masakichi Suzuki, and his violins

I was born in Nagoya in 1898 in the house of Masakichi Suzuki, founder of the largest violin factory in the world. It is an unchangeable fact beyond our control, strictly in God's hands, that no one can choose his parents. We cannot say, "I want to go over there; it is much more desirable, much better." Here or there, we cannot do a thing about it. It is absolutely fate—nothing else.

From the days of my father's grandfather, the Suzukis worked at home making Japanese samisens (three-stringed banjolike instruments). It was a side business for a poor samurai. My father, born in 1859 at the end of the Tokugawa era, eventually went to Edo (now Tokyo) to become an English-language teacher; but first he helped his family in making samisens. To have wanted to become an English teacher at the beginning of the Meiji period, he must have been a person with a considerably progressive spirit. In due time he became interested in Western musical instruments, beginning with a step-by-step research into the violin, which, he found, shared a common ancestor with the samisen. This was called a *rabanostron*. About five thousand years ago in ancient Egypt, when that country's culture thrived, one of these stringed instruments was laid beside the king in his tomb inside one of the pyramids. About four hundred years ago a Christian missionary played a viol, the antecedent of the violin, before Prince Nobunaga Oda at Otsu, Lake Biwa. But after the persecution and oppression of Christians by the Tokugawas, the sound of the violin was not heard in Japan until the reign of Meiji, when people became fond of the violin, and soon it was used generally. Although I say generally, there was scarcely a person who possesed an instrument when my father was a young man in Nagoya. By chance he found a teacher, at a teachers' college, who had one, and he begged, "Please let me examine your violin overnight while you are sleeping." That night he made a drawing of the instrument.

Ceaseless research

Then, in 1888, after a succession of failures, he made his first violin. There followed the foundation of the factory specializing in the production of violins, with constant improvement in quality. When things went well, he could turn out 400 violins and 4,000 bows a day. The Suzuki Violin Factory employed 1,100 workers, compared with the largest in Germany in Markneukirchen, which had 200. My father had not studied mechanics formally, yet he turned out fine machine-made instruments. He kept on with his own studies, and gave up his research only when he died, at the age of eighty-six. He then was in possession of twenty-one patents.

From childhood on, in our daily life, I learned countless things from my father, both morally and materially. Besides his ceaseless research and study, he taught me sincerity through his manner of living. Though his factory was very large, the business went into the red as a result of the world-wide depression of the twenties. Even now there are in Nagoya three streets in a row—Ume-machi, Uguisu-

machi, and Hayashi-machi, with Suzuki-cho running through them
in the center, leading to the Suzuki Violin Factory—that were all
laid out by my father, which show that Suzuki Violin once owned
much real estate and considerable property; but it all had to be sold
piece by piece to meet financial difficulties.

Sacrifices for the workers' sake

"I will be responsible for everyone. After all, the company, my
property too, was all built up through the efforts and cooperation
of my workers. I will not dismiss a single person as long as there
is anything left. I owe it to them." Thus my father spoke. Eventually we had to sell the mansion we lived in. And finally those
workers for whose future my father could make some sort of provi-
sion had to be let go. With the working force thus decreased, the
remaining ones moved into a smaller factory.

To people who had known the factory of former times, its suc-
cessor must have seemed very shabby and poor. But to my father
the object of an enterprise was not only money: it was a way of putting his high principles of life into action. The fact that the factory
flourished again after the war can be ascribed only to the heritage
of honesty and sincerity left by my father.

I liked fishing, and often used to go to the river to fish for *fun*,
the crucian carp. But at the end of a day of pleasant fishing I would
always return my fish to the water, as if to say, "Thank you for
giving me such happiness." I have never held the practical,
materialistic view that there is little use in doing something if there
are no immediate profits or results to show for it. My dreams are
for the future of mankind. And I will keep on trying to fulfill them,
plodding along patiently, earnestly, and with singleness of purpose.
Almost anything is possible of achievement in this way. It was my
father who planted the seed of this conviction in me.

An unfair advantage leads to evil

Whether a person is born into a rich family or a poor one is
beyond his control. It is a matter of fate. From the time I went to

primary school I used to play at the violin factory and listen to the conversation of the workmen; and when I was a junior-high-school student, my father always made me work at the factory during summer vacation. I shall never forget the joy of working there.

However, I was brought up more or less ignorant of the value of money. Perhaps that is why even if I am down to my last farthing, I somehow do not feel poor. In later years there were times when we could scrape together only a few yen, but I would come home in a taxi and be scolded by my family. I was never bothered in the least by the big stain in my studio ceiling caused by a leak in the roof. Shabby surroundings could not make me feel poor.

The post-World War I Germany in which I lived as a student was in the throes of the tremendous inflation that led to the rise of Hitler and World War II, and Berlin was filled with shady adventurers, both native and foreign. They would even accost a student like me: "There's a five-story building for sale. You can have it for only 10,000 yen. . . ." I always refused, saying that I was not in Germany to make money. But one day an old lady offered me a Guarnerius for only 2,000 yen. What an opportunity! But such things are not good. To my mind, irrespective of time or place, an unfair advantage leads only to evil.

Give money, do not lend it

One day a university professor who had helped me find lodgings and such came to see me. He said, "My wife and I have to take a trip home unexpectedly, and we haven't enough money available. I hesitate to ask you, but. . ." At that time the passage by sea for two was 2,000 yen; with another 500 yen for incidental expenses, they would be able to travel in comfort. I said I would lend it to them, and asked them to reimburse my father in Nagoya.

After the couple had sailed, I wrote to my father to explain what I had done and to get his approval. His reply took me aback: ". . . I sent you that money for your studies. I am shocked at your impertinence in lending it. In the future you are never to either lend or borrow money. . . if you have money enough to lend, it is better to share it, and share your friends' hardships too."

Lending the surplus money and considering that it would be all right if the money were returned to my father was juvenile thinking. On receiving my father's admonition, I determined never to lend money again. From that time on I have lived according to a certain plan. I decide how much money I need each month to live, and set it aside so that it may not be used for any other purpose. What is left is for myself and my friends. Many complications arise over money. But my father's injunction has saved me from them, and although my method may sound ridiculous, it has enabled me to get along without living beyond my means, without either taking advantage of friends or getting involved in unpleasant transactions with them.

Another thing my father taught me was an attitude of sociability and eagerness to learn from others. In those days most overland travel was done by train, and Father taught me that one should delight in the contacts one makes on journeys, for the people we meet and those who sit next to us or opposite us on trains or planes have been placed there by destiny. Therefore, greet them. It may lead to a conversation. Learn to be a good listener. The other person lives a quite different kind of life from you, and knows something you don't know, and you are bound to learn something. Rather than talking yourself, learn to draw the other person out, and above all listen. You will enjoy it. And the other person in turn will enjoy telling you about something he knows. Greetings, as I shall discuss later, are an important part of life; my father's precept that one should always say "How do you do" to people we come face to face with, even if we do not know them, is what formed the basis of my own thoughts and conduct with regard to pleasant human relations, humanity, love, harmony, improvement of one's fate, the grasping of opportunity, and so on.

Express gratitude, but do not ask for favors

One day a foreign priest I knew came to my house and said, "You should come to church and pray harder to enter the kingdom of heaven."

"No, Father," I replied, "I am no longer so presumptuous and irresponsible as to ask for the kingdom of heaven."

I did not mean, of course, that I did not want to go to heaven. It is just that I felt, as the poet Issa did, that "everything is in *your* hands, now at the end-of-year." It was through the music of Mozart that I learned to see it all so clearly. If I simply do my best, I cannot complain even if I am taken to hell. It is an extremely submissive attitude. I will help the church as much as I can, but I do not ask for anything in return. I can only say "Thank you" for everything I have received already.

It was my father who taught me this way of thinking.

When I was at junior high school, there was a time when four of the neighborhood children and I used to visit our local shrine every evening. We talked about all sorts of things on our way to and fro. That is all there was to it, but it was a pleasant daily task. Then one day my father asked me, "What do you say when you visit the shrine?" I replied that I asked for protection for all of my family. But my father remonstrated, "Stop being so selfish. When you go to the shrine each day, all you should say is 'Thank you very much!' " Since then, whatever holy place I visit I only express gratitude, saying, "Thank you very much." It is not right to offer a pittance in the way of alms and then ask for a great deal for oneself in return. I realized that what my father was trying to teach me was that although man is prone to always be waiting for something, that is wrong. I was seventeen at the time. Seventeen is a crucial time in a person's life. In my own life, as I am about to write, it was a memorable time indeed. By the age of seventeen or so, our previous "fate," or the things that have happened to us up to that time, have formed the basis on which our further fate begins to unfold. Of course, an accident or death or something unexpected may await us. One never knows what fate has in store. But I believe that it is managed from "over there," and that we over here can gain nothing by fear and worry, and should always have hope and live our lives to the best of our ability.

My introduction to Tolstoy

I consider that seventeen was the age at which my foundations were laid. In a manner of speaking it was the year I was born, the year I emerged as a human being. It was the year before I graduated from commercial school. About what happened to me I have told many people, and written many times, but if I leave it out now, I will not be able to explain my philosophy, so I shall repeat the story.

One day, as usual, I set off for my father's violin factory, where a thousand people were employed, and entered the office. I discovered an English typewriter, a novelty for me, and started punching the keys. Just then the chief of the export department came in and reprimanded me: "Master Shinichi, you mustn't type without paper in the machine."

"Oh, but I'm not really pushing the keys down," I promptly lied.

"Oh, I see," he replied simply, and went out. But he was hardly out of sight before I was filled with severe anger against myself, and contrition. "Coward," I thought; "why did I dissemble and not just apologize meekly?" I couldn't bear it any longer and went home. But I could not sit still. I went down to Hirokoji Street. I had to do something to get rid of my self-contempt. I went into a bookstore and looked around among some books on a shelf at random. After some time, fate led me to a copy of Tolstoy.

"The voice of conscience is the voice of God"

It was the small *Tolstoy's Diary*. I casually took it down from the shelf and opened it at random. My eyes fell on the following words: "To deceive oneself is worse than to deceive others." These harsh words pierced me to the core. It was a tremendous shock. I began to tremble with fear and could scarcely control myself. I bought the little book and rushed home. I devoured its contents. I read and reread that book so much that in the end it fell apart. What a marvelous man Tolstoy must have been! My admiration for him led me to immerse myself in all his writings. Tolstoy provided the staff of life on which I nurtured my soul. His *Diary* was always at my side. Wherever I went I took it with me. Several years later when, at twenty-three, I went to Germany to study, the book went with me in my pocket. Tolstoy said that one should not deceive oneself and that the voice of conscience is the voice of God. I determined to live according to these ideas.

Working, reading, and playing with children

I got so that I did only enough schoolwork to prevent my failing the examinations. I was fascinated with works that searched for the meaning of life, such as Bacon's essays and books on Western philosophy. And it probably was Tolstoy who started it all with me. I diligently studied the sayings of the priest Dogen entitled *Shushogi*, which begins: "It is the great Buddha Karma that illuminates life and lightens death. If the Buddha is in life and death, there is no life and death. . . ." I spent my time reading such books and working among the factory people until the sweat ran; my greatest joy was playing with the neighborhood children.

Later, I turned from the "conscience" of Tolstoy to follow the lead that Mozart provided in his music—the belief that it is the life force itself that is the whole basis of man's being, but I feel that the foundation of this thinking was laid in my seventeenth year. The image of young, growing children, who are the very essence of life's joy, took hold in my imagination then. That's how it all happened.

The origin of Talent Education

I played with children a lot in those days. The neighborhood children came running the minute they saw me in the distance approaching home. We used to take hands and go to my house, where they all played happily together with my younger sisters and brothers. I just liked children, that was all. And besides that, I had been inflamed by Tolstoy; I had learned to realize how precious children of four and five were, and wanted to become as one of them.

They have no thought of self-deception.
They trust people and do not doubt at all.
They know only how to love and know not how to hate.
They love justice and scrupulously keep the rules.
They seek joy, live cheerfully, and are full of life.
They know no fear and live in security.

I played with children so that I could learn from them. I wanted always to have the meekness of a child. A revolution was taking place within me. This is when the seed was sown of the Talent Education movement that was to be my life work.

Most of these beautiful children would eventually become adults filled with suspicion, treachery, dishonesty, injustice, hatred, misery, gloom. Why? Why couldn't they be brought up to maintain the beauty of their souls? There must be something wrong with education. That was when I first began to think along these lines.

A guiding principle

The motto of my alma mater, Nagoya Commercial School, was "First character, then ability." These words were inscribed on a tablet that hung in the lecture hall. This principle has been a light to my path all my life and is written on my heart. Fine scholars, artists, businessmen, and politicians alike succeed in their fields only if they are fine men. In order to succeed one must first be a person of fine character. From my freshman year on, until I graduated, four years later, I was class president. As I said before, I did not study very hard and so my marks were not very good, but I loved and respected everyone in my class and they all liked me, and they probably elected me because they knew I was obliging and loved to do things for people.

During the final examinations one of the students, whom I shall call A, was discovered by B to be cheating, and B announced the fact loudly to the teacher in charge. A was then sent out of the classroom, which was by then in an uproar. But when the examination was over and as soon as the students were out in the passage, another student, C, leaped upon informer B, a big boy, asking what kind of friend he thought he was, and hit him. The others joined in, and they all gave B a sound thrashing. I was still in the classroom. It all happened in the twinkling of an eye. Presently they sent for me, the class president, to come to the faculty room. "What is the meaning of this outrageous attack? Were you aware of it?"

"I was. I struck him too."

"What! Who are the students that struck him?"

"All the members of the class, sir."

"And you think you did right, do you?"

"I do not, sir. I think it was wrong to cheat, but it was extremely unfriendly to report him. Please punish us."

The whole school goes on strike

I went back to the classroom and told the students what I had said to the teacher, and I made a rash request. "What we did we had to do out of friendship. If you all agree, I'd like to say that it was sanctioned by all of us. And this year I want everyone to fail the examination."

Even those who had not taken part in the assault raised their hands, and we all agreed to stay for a fifth year. Presently each class member in turn was called into the faculty room and interrogated, and next morning when we arrived at school, there was a notice on the board announcing that twenty students would be punished, with indefinite suspension for ten, of whom my name headed the list, and a reprimand for the other ten. Although it apparently had been discovered that I had not been party to the assault, I was class president, and so it could not be helped. The other nine were the habitual roughnecks of the class.

Naturally some said this was unfair and that the punishment was unreasonable; others said they had taken part in the assault and why hadn't they been suspended? Protests were even made to the faculty. Complaints against the way the school was run spread throughout the students, and next day not a single person came to school. It was a sympathy strike.

The recess lasted for about a week, and then each student received a summons to appear at school. All the students, seventeen hundred strong, gathered in the auditorium, where the principal, Yoshiki Nishimura, the man who had created the motto "First character, then ability" and whom I admired beyond measure, spoke to us with tears in his eyes; he ended by saying that what had happened would all be forgotten and that the final examinations would be given again.

Normally there would have been two or three at least who failed, since it was not a particularly brilliant class, but as it was everybody passed and graduated. It seemed ironic. That was in 1916.

Evil should be punished

The night of the assault incident I told my father the whole story, and hanging my head, asked him to put me through school for another year, since I was about to fail. He smiled and simply said, "Well, it can't be helped, can it?" What a noble smile it was!

I believe the solution to the whole problem lay in my reply: I said that I recognized evil to be evil, explained my belief, and asked that we be punished. It must have been the seed of true friendship and love, as I had learned it from Tolstoy, taking root in my heart. I felt love for even the tiniest insect. On the path through the fields that I used on the way back from school to reach my house on the outskirts of Nagoya there were many ants, both large and small, busily going about their affairs. I remember being extremely careful not to step on any of them. When I thought that I could cause one of those tiny beings to lose its life forever, I could not walk carelessly. This is the sort of person I was as an early adolescent. It was not long after that I listened to records for the first time, and was amazed by Elman's "Ava Maria" and quite carried away by the sound of the violin.

Elman's recording moves my soul

I was brought up in the violin factory, and, at times, when I had a fight with my brothers and sisters, we would hit one another with violins. I then thought of the violin as a sort of toy.

When I was at primary school, work often went on at night in the handiwork department, as fifty or sixty workers polished the fronts and backs of violins. It was just about the time of the Russo-Japanese war of 1904–5. Each worker had an oil lamp hanging from the ceiling that shed light on his work. Every night after supper I would go to this manual-work section and listen spellbound as some of the workmen, whose names I still remember and who were marvelous storytellers, told of the stirring exploits of such heroes as

Iwami Jutaro and Kimura Shigenari. The picture of these workers spinning yarns as they worked with their hands under the light of the lamps, with a little boy raptly listening, is very nostalgic. Just as he would approach the climax, the storyteller would usually say, "Now, this is where a rice cake would taste good." Fearing that he might lose the thread of his story, I would race to our house next door and grab some pieces of *mochi* from the big keg in the kitchen. The storyteller would toast the *mochi* over a brazier nearby, go on with his polishing, and take up the fascinating tale once more.

After I entered commercial school, I used to spend the long summer vacation working at the factory. I learned all about violin making, from the mechanical work, the manual work, and the varnishing to the finished product. I learned the joy of working to one's utmost.

It must have been before I graduated from commercial college. Unexpectedly we got a gramophone. It was not electric, like the modern ones, but had to be wound by hand, and it had a horn as a loudspeaker. This horn was shaped like a morning glory and was big enough for a child to put its head inside. The first record I bought was Schubert's "Ave Maria" played by Mischa Elman. The sweetness of the sound of Elman's violin utterly enthralled me. His velvety tone as he played the medody was like something in a dream. It made a tremendous impression on me. To think that the violin, which I had considered a toy, could produce such beauty of tone!

Elman's "Ave Maria" opened my eyes to music. I had no idea why my soul was so moved. But at least I had already developed the ability to appreciate this beauty. My profound emotion was the first step in my search for the true meaning of art. I brought a violin home from the factory and, listening to Elman playing a Haydn minuet, I tried to imitate him. I had no score, and simply moved the bow, trying to play what I heard. Day after day I did this, trying to master the piece. My complete self-taught technique was more a scraping than anything else, but somehow I finally got so I could play the piece.

Haydn's minuet was thus my first "piece." Eventually I got so I derived great comfort from playing the violin, and became very fond of the instrument as well as developing deep love for music.

Fifty years of rising at five

At the violin factory the gates always opened at seven. From the point of view of the workers, not only my father but also we children were part of the management, and we weren't expected to get there before nine. But my first day at the factory, I thought, "Why I'm the same as the other workers. Why should I have managerial privileges?" It did not seem right from a purely human standpoint. All the others start at seven, and I shall do the same, I decided. I may have gotten the idea from Tolstoy too. I got up every morning at five. Then I would wake my brothers and sisters and take them for a walk to Tsurumi Park. There was a pond in the park, and the carp would make ripples on the water as they swam around eagerly waiting for us to bring them something to eat. After that we would hurry home and have our breakfast, and then I would leave for the factory. From the new house to which we had moved, one could walk to the factory in seventeen minutes. Even today I wake up at five. The habit I acquired of waking at five each morning during the twenty years I worked at the factory has remained with me for the past fifty years. At five in the evening, when working hours ended, I would start for home. One or another of the neighborhood children would be waiting for me. Swinging on my arms and hugging my legs, they could hardly wait to get to our house to play. I loved the violin, I loved my work, I loved talking and playing with the children. Those were happy days indeed. Did I not experience any discontent at all, you ask? I think I can truthfully say that I had no complaints at all against the world around me.

But I was discontented with myself. I scolded myself continually, and was always aware of things about myself that I wanted to improve. I had not the slightest desire to complain about members of my family exercising their management privilege of arriving at the factory late. The laborers started work early in the morning; that was why I felt I too must do so. It was the voice of conscience— "The voice of conscience is the voice of God." I wanted to put Tolstoy's words into practice. Whether it was that I was following my conscience or that I felt a sense of completeness, I was very happy. That is why I was able to enjoy the trip to Chishima so much.

Toward the end of that trip, when Marquis Tokugawa said to me, "Why don't you study music instead of working at the violin factory?" and Miss Koda agreed, saying, "Yes, why don't you?" it didn't seem that they were talking about me at all. I was working at the factory because my father wanted me to help him with administration, and I couldn't expect him to change his plans. And anyway, I was happy with my work.

I wasn't thinking of becoming a musician at all. I had been tremendously impressed by Elman, but I was interested only in discovering more about what art really is. It is only because I wanted to discover this that I played about with the violin. But. . .

I stay in Marquis Tokugawa's mansion

The autumn after the summer cruise to northern Chishima, Marquis Tokugawa came to Nagoya one day to visit us. He asked my father what he thought about my studying music, saying that Miss Koda had said that I showed promise. I was sure my father would probably say: "He may like music, but he doesn't need to work where he will be obliged to kowtow to a lot of people in order to get on. If he wants to listen to music, he can become a successful businessman and hire those kind of people to come and play for him." That is the way my father used to think at one time. My father being like that, I was sure he wouldn't agree.

But since it was Marquis Tokugawa who asked him, he could not say no. As I said earlier, Marquis Tokugawa brought about the most unexpected change in my fate. The following spring, when I was twenty-one, I went to Tokyo and studied the rudiments of the violin with Ko Ando, the younger sister of Miss Koda. I was given a room in Marquis Tokugawa's mansion in Fujimi-cho, Azabu. I had actually intended to buy a house to live in, but the plan had failed and the Marquis kindly invited me to stay at his mansion, which was a stroke of good fortune and a golden opportunity. I became even closer to the Marquis, and since I had my meals with him, he told me a great many things. Also, almost every day at the Tokugawa mansion, there would be visits from scholars and friends, such as the physicist Torahiku Terada and the phoneticist Kotoji Sat-

suda. I was in the midst of fine men such as these. I'm sure it was
Marquis Tokugawa's subtle way of seeing that my character was
properly trained.

The graduation recital at Ueno Academy is a great disappointment

I had a weekly violin lesson from Miss Ando. She suggested that
I enroll the following year at the music academy in Ueno, for, as
she said, I could study other things there too. I was already plan-
ning to take the entrance examination and was preparing myself for
it. As the day of the examination approached, at Miss Ando's sug-
gestion I went to hear the graduation recital at Ueno. I was frightfully
disappointed. I had gone with such great expectations. The next day
I went to see Miss Ando; I told her, "I heard the graduation recital
last night. If that's the best I can do after studying at Ueno, I do
not want to take the entrance examination. I would rather go on
studying with you, if I may." Hearing the graduation recital after
having been listening only to the best performers of the world on
records left me feeling quite disillusioned and despondent. I thought
it far better not to enter the academy at all. Miss Ando smiled. "All
right, if that's what you prefer. But you'll have to work hard." So
I started lessons with her again once a week. Unexpectedly, my not
entering the Ueno Music Academy led to my going to Germany.

My destiny beckons

Besides my lessons with Miss Ando, I took private lessons in
musical theory from Professor Ryutaro Hirota and in acoustics from
Professor H. Tanabe. After I had been living in Tokyo for about
a year and a half, Marquis Tokugawa began talking about taking
a world tour. "Suzuki," he said, "why don't you come too? It will
take about a year, but it will be fun." I had just started studying
the violin. I thought I was a bit too young to benefit from a world

tour at this stage of my life, and I said so. So the matter was dropped, and it was agreed that I should work hard at my violin. But soon after that my summer vacation started, and one day, at home, I mentioned the proposed tour to my father.

His reply was unexpected: "Why, that's an excellent idea." As I looked up he continued. "If you were with the Marquis, I shouldn't worry about you at all. It would be a good idea for you to have a look at the world. You can probably go round the world for 150,000 yen. Go along and keep the Marquis company." But even though my father thought it a good opportunity, I refused. I didn't want to give up the studies I had only just begun.

That September, after summer holidays were over, one evening at dinner I told Marquis Tokugawa what my father had said. Holding his chopsticks in midair, he looked at me with a twinkle in his eye. "Well done, Shinichi. You'd better grab that 150,000 yen. You can stop off in Germany and study violin. What a good idea! Next time I go to Nagoya I'll have a word with your father."

Marquis Tokugawa completely sold my father on his ingenious scheme. My father apparently said, "I am delighted to have you take my son with you, sir. By all means let him study in Germany with whatever money is left over." It's a cliché, I know, but one really has no idea what fate has in store for one. Though disappointed with the Ueno Music Academy in the spring, by autumn I was on board the luxury liner *Hakone Maru* en route to Marseilles. My father thought I was on a world tour, but I was really on my way to Germany to study. It was October, 1920, and I was twenty-two.

There was tremendous inflation in Germany at the time, so my money went a long way. At first I was able to get 600 marks for 10 yen, and finally 100,000,000 marks. It cost me, of course, more than 150,000 yen in the end, since I ended up spending eight years in Germany.

It certainly was not I who opened the door of my destiny. I felt that something was always leading me. What led me then was Marquis Tokugawa's great love. I always tried to follow like a child, and because of this he never failed to push me and give me the encouragement I needed. It was Tolstoy who taught me this meekness. So it was Tolstoy who opened up my destiny.

The soul of art: Klingler,
the teacher I chose myself

Recently at Christmas a small parcel came from Germany to our
house in Matsumoto. It was from Professor Klingler, who lived in
Munich and who, at the ripe age of eighty, still composed and was
active in music. It was a sonata he had written for unaccompanied
violin. Recollecting my revered teacher of more than forty years
before, I was carried back to my days as a student in Berlin and
became lost in reverie.

I had said good-bye to Marquis Tokugawa, who was going on
a world tour, at his suite at Marseilles, and had gone straight to Berlin
with Mr. Fiegel, a German engineer I had become friendly with on
board the *Hakone Maru*. I then took a room at a hotel, and for
three months I went to concerts every day. I had refused Professor
Ando's offer to provide me with an introduction to a teacher. I went
to hear everybody, from famous performers to rising young artists,
for I wanted to find someone of whom I could truly say, "This is
the man I want for a teacher." But at the end of three months I
still had not found him. Just as I was on the point of moving to
Vienna, I heard the Klingler Quartet. They were playing at the Sing
Academy. It was Mrs. Kapel, a distant relative of Fiegel's, who took
me there. I can still vividly remember the sound of their performance
that night. It was music of profound spirituality. It completely
charmed my soul with its beauty, and it spoke to me gently. At the
same time it had superb order and technique. Without any introduction and, in English, since as yet I could not write German, I wrote,
"Please take me as your pupil."

No sooner had I sent the letter than I heard discouraging predic-
tions from Japanese musicians in Germany. They assured me that
I had no chance, because Klingler didn't take private pupils. The
following Wednesday, however, I received an answer from Klingler
saying, "Come." My experience was exactly the same as that of Koji
Toyoda many years later, who, at the age of nineteen, approached
Enesco on his own and became his pupil. Asking the way to his house
through the strange and unfamiliar streets of Berlin, I visited Klingler,

and he asked me to play the Rode concerto. I made a mistake at one point and had to play the passage over again. "This is the end," I thought hopelessly, but he said, "When can you come again?"

A courageous man of moral strength and truth

Thus it was that I began to study with a teacher of my own choosing. I was Professor Klingler's only private pupil. Klingler was about forty, handsome, and a man one could become extremely fond of. What he taught me was not so much technique as the real essence of music. For instance, if we were working on a Handel sonata, he would earnestly explain to me what great religious feeling Handel must have been filled with when he wrote it, and then he would play it for me. He would look for the roots underlying a man and his art and lead me to them. To be led by a man of such high character was indeed a blessing for me.

His friends were all wonderful people too. He often invited me to concerts at his home. It is impossible to evaluate how much these taught me. When the Nazis began to flourish and Hitler rose to power, I was back in Japan, and news came to me that vividly reminded me what a courageous man Klingler was. In front of the main entrance of the Berlin Music Academy was a statue of the great late-nineteenth-century German violinist Joseph Joachim, a Jew. Hitler ordered it removed. Klingler alone fearlessly defended this statue of the man who not only had been his teacher but had rendered such great services in the cause of art. "You shall not destroy it," he declared. Professor Klingler was expelled from the music academy. His was the greatness of a true artist. From Klingler, who had courage such as this, I learned a great deal about moral strength.

I learn what art really is

I would play the piece I had been given by Professor Klingler, and he would correct me. The lesson would usually last two hours. He would always assign several pieces at once, so that I gradually covered a great variety of material. I believe he used this diversified method of study in order to try to correct my faults. He never seemed to grudge the amount of time he spent on me. But to me, who tended to be rather lazy, it was always a tremendous ordeal just having to play through so many pieces. As I have said before, I had no illusions about my performing ability. But I did not know that my despair was brought about not because I had no talent but because I did not know how to develop it. I did not know that it was just a matter of repeating a piece hundreds of times in order to play it better, more nobly, and more beautifully. But I learned from Klingler the essence of what art truly is. My ultimate desire was not to become a performer but to understand art. And in that respect I learned a tremendous amount from Klingler. The first four years we studied concertos and sonatas, and the next four years chamber music. This was because I had gradually become extremely fond of chamber music, as well as that Professor Klingler was a great master of this medium.

I was doing what I wanted to do.

Dr. Einstein becomes my guardian

When I decided to stay in Berlin and study with Klingler, I took lodgings in the house of a gray-haired widow and her elderly maid. Both the landlady and the maid were hard of hearing, so they did not complain no matter how loudly I practiced the violin. Besides this stroke of luck, I had the good fortune of knowing Dr. Michaelis, a professor of medicine, and his family, who were very kind to me. When the professor was in Japan, he had often been invited to our house, and so he was especially kind to me. When he received an invitation to go to America to become dean of Johns Hopkins University, he said to me, "I shall no longer be able to look after you, and so I have asked a friend of mine to keep an eye on you." The friend turned out to be Dr. Albert Einstein, who developed the theory of relativity.

Thus, unexpectedly, I experienced the warm friendship of this world-famous scholar and the outstanding people of his circle. This was one of the most wonderful things that happened to me in my whole life. It provided in later years the conviction and basic theory behind the driving force that enabled me to carry out without the slightest doubt my Talent Education movement for small children. My contact with the greatness of Dr. Einstein as a man began in the following way.

"People are all the same, madame"

Before Dr. Michaelis went to America, he gave a dinner party, after which there was some music. I was asked to play too. I was not very good, but they insisted, so I submitted and played a piece I liked—a Bruch concerto I was studying with Klingler at the time. When we were drinking tea afterward, there was a quiet conversation. "I really can't understand it," began an elderly lady of about seventy who was sitting right in front of Dr. Einstein. "Suzuki grew up in Japan in a completely different environment from ours. But in spite of that his performance clearly expressed to me the Germanness of Bruch. Tell me, is such a thing possible?" After a brief interval Dr. Einstein, young enough to be her son, said quietly, "People are all the same, madame." I was tremendously moved.

Men of science but virtuosos, too

Often when there was a good concert, Dr. Einstein would telephone me and say, "I have tickets, so let's go."

The violinist Busch (1891–1952) was a good friend of his, and Einstein spoke highly of him both as a person and as a performer. Before Busch's concert Einstein telephoned to tell me what time to meet him at the bus stop. I was careful to get to the stop on time, but the eminent scholar was there before me. Even though I was a mere stripling, he had invited me as his guest and treated me accordingly. I just bowed, and did not know what to do.

Dr. Michaelis was an accomplished pianist. He used to accompany his wife, who had studied singing at the Vienna Music Academy. Once, at a home concert, his wife whispered to him to please play half a tone lower because she had a bit of a cold. "Yes,

dear," he replied and without a moment's hesitation played the ac-
companiment a semitone lower. Moreover, it was a difficult song
by Brahms, and he was playing without the music. I was really
astonished. Like Dr.. Schweitzer, who had difficulty choosing between being a professional musician or being a doctor, Dr. Michaelis
had been torn between music and medicine.

Einstein was an acknowledged virtuoso on the violin. He never
went anywhere without his violin. His specialties, such as the Bach
Chaconne, were magnificent—his light, flowing finger movements,
his beautifully delicate tone. In comparison with his playing, mine,
though I tried to keep in mind that I must play effortlessly and with
ease, seemed to me a constant struggle.

Young Kaufmann's impromptus

Although they did not tell it to me in so many words, Michaelis,
the physician, and Einstein, the scientist, graphically brought home
to me what the study of music can do for a person. But before I
say anything more on this subject, I should like to tell of one more
unforgettable experience. One evening at Einstein's house there was
music after dinner. At that time I had an eighteen-year-old friend
who was studying composition at the music academy. (When I was
eighteen, I had only just started teaching myself to play the violin.)

"Tonight we shall have some impromptu music by Kaufmann.
Here—" Einstein played a short theme on the piano.

Kaufmann stood up and said, "I will begin with an early composer. Here is a fugue in the style of Bach." I was amazed. He im-
provised on Einstein's theme with sureness and fluency, not only using Bach's harmonies but in a style clearly reminiscent of Bach
himself.

After the Bach-style fugue was over, someone said, "What about
Chopin next?"

"All right; now I shall play in the style of Chopin," he said,
and began a nocturne of Einstein's same theme. The theme became
beautifully Chopinesque in an animated performance that flowed
along like a stream of sadness. In the same way he went on to pro-

duce beautiful music in the styles of Brahms, Beethoven, Johann Strauss, and Mahler. This sort of thing cannot be done unless one is thoroughly familiar with many composers and their styles. And the fact that he could improvise without the slightest hesitation showed what confidence and musicianship young Kaufmann had.

Whether Kaufmann's amazing skill at improvising would lead to his becoming a great composer or not is beside the point. I was deeply impressed by his talent, and it struck me that this kind of skill could be developed. What a delight it would be!

Not only Einstein but all the members of his intimate circle were prominent people in their fields. They all loved art and were extremely modest and kind. Here I was, just a beginner of no particular talent, a mere struggling student, and never once did they make me feel foolish or treat me lightly, but they accepted me warmly and made sure I enjoyed myself. I was touched by the considerate way they took pains to include me in their conversation and to see that I was not bored.

Harmony—in order to achieve it, one person must gracefully give in to the other, and it is nobler to be the one who gives in than the one who forces the other to give in. Harmony cannot be achieved any other way. It was things like that that I learned from Einstein and the people who gathered at his house.

People who can get together and make music. . . .

I want Japanese children to grow up to be people who have this pleasure in their lives and to be people of as high intellect and sensitivity as those people in Berlin. That is what I want. The purpose of Talent Education is to train children, not to be professional musicians but to be fine musicians and to show high ability in any other field they enter. Dr. Michaelis is a case in point. Somewhere I have heard the phrase, "The matchless beauty of Einstein's mathematics." I am sure this beauty of conception was the outcome of pure musical skill. Einstein was only sixteen when he had the idea that was to bring about such a revolution in the science of physics, and he himself says, "It [the optics of motion] occurred to me by intuition. And music is the driving force behind this intuition. My parents had me study the violin from the time I was six. My new discovery is the result of musical perception."

Thus my eight years in Berlin were happily spent in the company of people of high intellect, sensitivity, and good will. I also met my future wife at one of those home concerts, and we were married before the eight years I spent in Berlin were over.. . . And while the great numbers of performances I listened to by European musicians filled me with despair as to my own performing ability, they gradually brought me nearer to an understanding of what art really is.

The concerts I attended in Berlin are replete with memories. Each one is still vivid in my mind, and time only serves to distill and clarify the memories even further. Glazunov conducting his own composition with the Berlin Philharmonic. . . the lady violinist Cecila Hansen, who played the concerto. . . the beautifully grand way the great composer Richard Strauss used to conduct . . . the concert at which Mascagni conducted a chorus of one thousand . . . Busoni's piano playing that made one think of the sweet, lovely fragrance of white lilies in the garden at eventide; when Busoni played on it, the piano in Berlin Philharmonic Hall sounded like a different instrument, with a marvelously tender sound through which Beethoven would speak to us warmly out of his loneliness. . . the Sunday concert series in which dignified Schnabel played all the Beethoven sonatas. . . . Furtwängler, whom I went to hear so often—he was the regular conductor of the Berlin Philharmonic. . . . At a concert of the Contemporary Music Society, which used to introduce contemporary music from all over the world, I remember being intensely impressed by the modern musical expression of Schönberg's symphonic poem "Pelleas and Melisande."

But among all these what captivated me most was the performance of Mozart's music one night at the Sing Academy by the Klingler Quartet. The whole program that evening was Mozart. And when it came to the Clarinet Quintet (A major, K.581), something happened to me that had never happened before. I felt as though I had lost the use of my arms.

I am captivated by eternal love

It was Mozart who taught me to know perfect love, truth, goodness, and beauty. And I now deeply feel as if I were under direct orders from Mozart, and he left me a legacy; in his place I am to further the happiness of all children. What led to this revelation was the Klingler Quartet's playing of Mozart's Clarinet Quintet.

That evening I seemed to be gradually drawn into Mozart's spirit, and, finally I was not conscious of anything else, not even of my own being, I became so immersed. Of course, I did not realize this until afterward. After the performance I tried to applaud. But there was no feeling from the shoulders down, and I could not move either hand. I don't know when the clapping stopped. During the applause I just sat there in a trance. Finally I got my hands back, but even when the feeling came back, I still just stared into space. An indescribable, sublime, ecstatic joy had taken hold of my soul. I had been given a glimpse of Mozart's high spiritual world. Through sound, for the first time in my life, I had been able to feel the highest pulsating beauty of the human spirit, and my blood burned within me. It was a moment of sublime eternity when I, a human being, had gone beyond the limits of this physical body. That night I couldn't sleep at all. Mozart, the man, had shown me immortal light.

Filled with the joy of love, I give up sadness

It happened in Berlin when I was twenty-four. From that day until now I have received power and strength from Mozart. I am eternally a child on Mozart's bosom. What I never cease to marvel at in Mozart's music is his superhuman love. It is a great tenderness and love felt only by the soul. And this love takes cognizance of man's deep sorrow. . . birth and death. . . the evanescence and loneliness of life. . .the all-pervasive sadness. This sadness Mozart expressed not only with the minor scale but with the major scale as well, in the midst of his deep love. For man both life and death are the inescapable business of nature. There is in Mozart's music a clear vision of this inevitability.

That piercing sadness pervades the major mode of the Clarinet Quintet. Let me give you the beginning of the second movement—

However, Mozart does not simply resign himself to this sad life that has no satisfactory solution. That is where his great love comes in. Although he is aware of sadness, Mozart answers life with a loving affirmative. That is why it is possible to go beyond despair, to envelop the situation in love and change it and bring about the joy of living.

When I listen to Mozart, he seems to envelop me in his great love. Mozart's love for mankind is not merely a pious kind of love that points to hope in the next world through religious ecstasy: "All right. Life is sad. But if there is love, see how beautiful life can be. The sad life that we all must live—let us go along together and comfort one another."

This is what Mozart says to us, and I affirm it with all my heart.

Recently I have been studying the works of the Japanese poet Issa, and I understand the mind of Mozart even more clearly. Haiku such as these, which Issa wrote in his fifties, are pure Mozart:

> *Be it as it may,*
> *All my life is in your hands,*
> *Now at the end-of-year.*

> *Though I am aware*
> *Evening bells my curfew toll,*
> *I enjoy the cool.*

"In your hands" expresses the great soul of Buddhism, I believe. It does not mean that if there is nothing to hope for in the after-life, it matters not whether you work or not in this one. It means that no human being knows what his future life holds. It means that in spite of the sadness, love can make this life happy.

People who are optimistic, happy, and cheerful, even though they are only so on the surface, being always conscious of the ephemerality of life and how infinitesimal their existence must seem in relation to the universe—when people like that are asked what life really means, they must answer with Mozart: "I live in the love of everyone. Only this life is worth living."

That we are born and that we finally die is the work of Mother Nature. It is not the responsibility of each one of us. Each human being has only the responsibility for living. That is my view of life. And I pray that my life may be lived in the midst of love and joy. No one essentially seeks hatred and misery. Children are examples of life in its truest form, for they really try to live in pure love and joy. I cannot live without children. But I love grownups too because I feel a great sympathy for them—"After all, these people too must die." Men's lives should consist in loving one another, in comforting one another. Mozart teaches this, and I believe it.

It is in our power to educate all the children of the world to become a little better as people, a little happier. We have to work toward this. I ask no more than the love and happiness of mankind, and I believe that this is what everyone really wants.

Love can be had only by loving. Our life is worth living only if we love one another and comfort one another. I searched for the meaning of art in music, and it was through music that I found my work and my purpose in life. Once art to me was something far off, unfathomable and unattainable. But I discovered it was a tangible thing. Anybody who takes up an art is apt to think of the object of his ambition as something very far off, and I tried to search for the secret. But after my eight years in Germany, I found that it was not at all what I had imagined it to be.

The real essence of art turned out to be not something high up and far off. It was right inside my ordinary daily self. The very way one greets people and expresses oneself is art. If a musician wants to become a fine artist, he must first become a finer person. If he does this, his worth will appear. It will appear in everything he does, even in what he writes. Art is not in some far-off place. A work of art is the expression of a man's whole personality, sensibility, and ability.

As I have said, on one hand I listened constantly to fine works in fine performances, immersing myself in Mozart; on the other hand, I was exposed to the modesty, high intellectual sensibility, and humanity of Dr. Einstein and his group; and in this way I came to the end of my search and realized what art truly is. After I found out, the rest was up to me. It was up to me to polish and refine myself, that was all. Then why is one so moved by music? I will try to explain.

If you think of doing something, do it

Of what use is knowledge by itself?. . .

One morning in 1953 a newspaperman telephoned me to say that Jacques Thibaud was dead. The plane in which he was riding had crashed in the Alps. I was so shocked that I was hardly able to coherently give the reporter the impression of the great man that he sought from me. I just stood there holding the receiver. It was like irreplaceably losing someone near and dear. After the first shock the following thoughts came to me as I quietly wept. I had never met Thibaud, but he had been living in my heart for some time. I loved his playing and admired him intensely. Having listened to his recordings for twenty-odd years, I could sense his personality, and had been studying his expression and way of playing. Music . . . through sound. Thibaud had come to life in my soul and fostered in me an ineradicable love and admiration. Music . . . sound, tone. What strange things they are, I realized at that moment. Man does not live in intellect. Man lives in the wonderful life force. "Sound has life and soul without form." That is when I thought of the words that are now my motto.

Fifty years ago it was Tolstoy's "Conscience is the voice of God," and to live in conscience was my sacred creed. But now "conscience" has changed to "life."

Music, the language of life

One must submit to the demands of life—but what exactly *is* life? The life we try to live is always a search for happiness. Very few people seek wisdom. Children in their simplicity seek what is true, what is good, what is beautiful, based on love. That, I believe, is "the true nature of man" as described by Gautama Buddha. Mozart, whose music taught me the simple love and joy that overcome misery, must have believed that too. And it was Thibaud who taught me that our life force is the greatest thing we have.

When the human race created the culture of speech and writing, it also produced the sublime culture called music. It is a language that goes beyond speech and letters—a living art that is almost mystical. This is where its emotional impact comes in. Bach, Mozart, Beethoven—without exception they live clearly and palpably in their music, and speak forcefully to us, purifying us, refining us, and awakening in us the highest joy and emotion.

> *He is young as a youth, yet wise as an old man.*
> *Never old-fashioned, never newfangled.*
> *Buried, yet all the more*
> *Sprightly and full of life.*
> *And his kindly smile*
> *Shines on us and purifies us.*
> *Never more so than now. . .*

These words are part of a poem written by the pianist Busoni describing the personality and philosophy, the sadness, the love and noble-mindedness of Mozart as communicated to us in his music.

Talent education is life education

Mother Nature gives every one of us the potential to live this kind of life. But the life force is beyond human intellect. If people only realized what a marvelous thing it is, they would have greater respect for it, and appreciate it in children, in adults, in themselves.

Pablo Casals deeply moves us with his performances, and he in turn weeps with emotion at the performance of children that brings tears to so many eyes. The deep emotion in each case is caused by the great and beautiful symphony of life in its purest state. The human heart, feeling, intellect, behavior, even the activity of organs and nerves—all are but part of the life force. We must not forget that man is the embodiment of life force, and that it is the power of the life force that controls human seeking and finding. That is why Talent Education has to be an education that is directed to this life force.

Education rather than instruction

Why do all children possess the marvelous ability to speak their mother tongue quite effortlessly? Therein lies the secret of how to educate all human ability. Schools instruct and train as hard as they can, without good results. There must be something wrong in their method. My thirty years of experience makes me firmly believe this. With the emphasis put only on informing and instructing, the actual growing life of the child is ignored. There has been no thorough research into how ability is acquired. The word education implies two concepts: to educe, which means to "bring out, develop from latent or potential existence" *(Concise Oxford Dictionary)*, as well as to instruct. But the emphasis in schools is only on the instruction aspect, and the real meaning of education is totally forgotten.

Even in primary school beginners are merely instructed, or informed of certain things, and then assailed by test after test to see how much they remember, and on the basis of their tests fateful pronouncements are made: "This child is superior," "This child needs admonishment," "This child was born with a poor brain."

Grading cannot be done by test. Tests can only determine how much the children have understood and whether there are any who have not understood. Should not the examination paper be used only as a means of finding out which questions the child does not understand and which problems the child cannot do? Actually, these results would show the teacher's ability rather than the child's. But unfortunately in today's schools it is invariably the child who is graded on tests.

The object of sending a child to primary school should not be just the assessment of his ability by tests. Nevertheless, the aim of schools today seems to be only the assessment of mankind, of children, and the only thing that seems to be important is scholastic rank. I think this is quite wrong.

If it does nothing else, the nine years of compulsory education ought to instill at least one superior skill in each child. It needn't be a school subject. For instance, if it were daily inculcated in a child to be kind to people in daily life, whether in school, in friendships, or at home, what a happy society could be created! But education today simply teaches the maxim, "Be kind." The world is full of intellectuals who are very well aware that "one should be kind to people" but who are, in fact, unhappy egoists. Today's society is the result of this sort of education. I want—if I can—to get education changed from mere instruction to education in the real sense of the word—education that inculcates, brings out, develops the human potential, based on the growing life of the child. That is why I am devoting all my efforts to furthering Talent Education; what a child becomes depends entirely on how he is educated. My prayer is that all children on this globe may become fine human beings, happy people of superior ability, and I am devoting all my energies to making this come about, for I am convinced that all children are born with this potential.

To merely "want" to do something is not enough

Life was wretched in Japan right after the end of World War II. The winters in Matsumoto are severe, and there are days when the temperature falls to 13 or 18 degrees below zero centigrade. On one of those days my sister returned from an errand, and, as she shook off the snow, she said, "In all this cold, there is a wounded soldier standing on the bridge down by Hon-machi, begging. He is standing there shivering in this driving snow, and nobody is putting any money in the box at his feet . . . I wanted to invite him in to sit in our *kotatsu* in our warm room and give him some tea."

I immediately replied, "You merely *wanted* to?"

She answered yes, and suddenly ran out into the street. I made the room warmer, stirred up the fire in the *kotatsu*, got out some cookies somebody had sent us as a gift, and waited. About thirty minutes later my sister came back with the white-clad, wounded soldier. "This lady insisted—" he began to explain.

"You are very welcome; do come in." Koji and I urged him into the *kotatsu* with us, and we sat and talked about all sorts of things.

Finally he asked me for the second time, "Why are you so kind to me?"

"My sister happened to see you," I replied, "and insisted on inviting you in."

"It's the first time any one has . . . and today was so cold and miserable," he said.

One must be able to put things into practice

He told us about his experience in the war, and how he was going from place to place collecting money for the wounded soldiers, and we talked and talked for three hours, until he got warm again. He then got up, saying he had to go to Nagano. At the front door, in spite of his protestations that I already had been far too kind, I put some money in his box, saying jokingly that it was just compensation for causing him to lose a half day's business, and anyway it was not his own personal box and so he had no right to refuse.

Afterward my sister said to me, "You taught me an excellent lesson." Indeed, it was our first exercise in "If you want to do something, do it."

Plenty of people often think, "I'd like to do this, or that." We all have the ability to think that. But it usually ends there, and people who put their thoughts into practice are very few indeed. I realized I was one of those people who just think of doing things, and I made a resolution: "There is no merit in just thinking about doing something. The result is exactly the same as not thinking about it. It is only doing the thing that counts. I shall acquire the habit of doing what I have in mind to do."

Why is it that so many people think of doing things and do not do them? Why do they not have the power to put into practice the things they think of doing? *If one just thinks about it, the chance slips by.* From the time they are children, people are ordered about by their parents to do this, to do that. They develop resistance, and reluctantly do as they are told, or avoid doing it if possible. The resistance habit becomes subconscious, until they are unable to perform immediately even those things they think of doing themselves. They may think something is a good thing to do, but they have gotten so that they are unable to do it simply and naturally. People lose a great deal this way.

"We should have done it. It was such a good chance, but we let it slip by." Because they are incapable of putting thoughts into action straight away time after time, people's destiny never develops. They close the stable door after the horse is gone. Chances come to everyone. Yes, chances come; but we don't grasp them. By not claiming them we renounce them.

"I should write a letter"—"I should reply to a letter." If you think so, write immediately. You are not doing anything at the time but just think you will wait and do it later. Even small tasks should not be neglected, but completed right away. It is very important to be able to do this. People who get a lot done manage it because they have the ability to get each necessary thing done right there and then. If you put a task off until some other time, you will never get it done, because "some other time" has its own tasks. Consequently you end up doing nothing and become a person who keeps putting things off. Time doesn't wait; but most people are so *narigachi na no desu* (not up to doing things).

The habit of action—this, I think, is the most important thing we must acquire. Life's success or failure actually depends on this one thing. So what should we do? We should get so that it is second nature to put our thoughts into action. Start now, today. True, it is easier to say than to do, but the more you do it, the more of a habit it will become. It is an indispensable skill. To know something and not to put it into practice is a weak point, but knowledge is mere knowledge, and is not to be confused with ability and skill. Not until knowledge becomes an inseparable part of one is it an ability or skill. There are plenty of people who know a lot about baseball and can criticize a game; however, the spectator lacks the intuitive skill, judgment, and physical coordination of the experienced player.

A fine society is not built by people who just think about what is right to do. What we need is people with the ability of the experienced baseball player, people with various deeply inculcated skills.

How to develop new skills

Action cannot be separated from thought. People with fine judgment are people of ability. Reflective thought is part of judgment.

Naturally, the finer the person, the greater his ability to think constructively. In training oneself, the road to improvement is closed if thoughtful self-examination is lacking. They say, "Happy are the thinkers." But unfortunately, in most cases it is "Unhappy are the thinkers." Why? Because thought is often just idle thought, and does not include self-correction. What is the use of pouring repentance on repentance? Too much thought makes thought meaningless, and finally we get so we reject thought altogether. Self-examination not accompanied by change is the same as not putting into action what we think of doing. Self-training is extremely difficult. If the ability is not developed, the power of self-examination, which should be a light to our feet, goes out altogether. We must cultivate thought, or rather self-correction. But how is it done? I have come to the following conclusions about self-correction as applied in music. Rather than theorizing, let me give you an example of how I trained a child who could not sing in tune—who, in other words, was tone-deaf—acquire an accurate ear. It is the key to how the change may be achieved.

Most tone-deaf children cannot produce the first four notes of the scale, do, re, mi, fa, without making the semitone interval, fa, a little too high. That is, they have already acquired the habit of making fa too high. This "pre-education" cannot be changed, as I found out. Then what does one do? I found that one has to teach them a new fa. If they have learned the wrong fa by hearing it five thousand times, one must make them listen to the right fa six thousand or seven thousand times. At first there are no results, but after hearing the right fa three thousand, then four thousand times, and when the number reaches five and six thousand times, the ability to produce the correct fa acquired by listening to it six thousand times begins to take precedence over the ability to produce the wrong fa that was acquired by listening only five thousand times. A new function has been developed. Success is now ours. Just as left-handed people find it easier to use their left hand than their right hand, one always prefers to do the thing one can do best. The right fa became easier and more natural for that child, so in the end he always produces it. The result is that he is no longer tone deaf. It takes six or seven months to achieve this with a child of six.

This is the way to replace a wrong skill with a right one. As I said before it is not a question of correction but a question of developing a new skill to take the place of the wrongly acquired one.

Speaking of such experiments, if you take a child of six away from his home, where he has been brought up speaking the Osaka dialect, and place him where Tokyo Japanese is spoken, then by the time he is sixteen—ten years later—he will have acquired a perfect Tokyo accent. It is the same as curing the tone-deaf child. The Osaka dialect has not been "corrected"; the child will just have acquired the new skill of speaking Tokyo Japanese, and it will be more deeply rooted in his consciousness than the Osaka dialect.

Well, then, let us go back to the question of putting thought into action. I began by saying that self-correction is difficult even with self-examination, and then I went on to describe a case showing that one does not correct, but develops a new skill. As you have probably guessed, thought, to be profitable, must immediately be followed by correct action, in order to acquire a new habit better than the habit that one has already. Unless this is done, the self-examination gets no further than thought. No matter what, progress cannot be made without the acquiring of new skills. Unless accompanied by action, no amount of thought or self-examination will do any good. Therefore it is essential to acquire the habit of action, of putting things into practice. Any skill can be acquired by constant repetition. This golden rule can be applied right now. Anything you think of doing, however insignificant, should be done immediately. Spur yourself on and carry it through without becoming discouraged. If this becomes an ingrained habit, things you thought were impossible will become possible, and closed doors will open, as you will discover in many ways.

The old saying, "If you try it, you can do it," is not so simple as it sounds, but don't dismiss it as something that does not concern you. It concerns us all.

Memory training—vital to talent education

The curriculum at the Talent Education infant school differs from that of ordinary kindergartens. It aims at taking preschool children and molding them into superior human beings. Basic skills are taught that will help them acquire other skills later. Teachers of high artistic sensibility and fine character teach them calligraphy, drawing, English conversation, and so on; it is my hope that the children will unconsciously acquire from being with these teachers some of their fine human qualities.

It is amazing what strong, beautiful calligraphy these preprimary school children produce with only a little training. An art exhibition is also part of the curriculum, and the pictures our children produce are remarkable. The numberals too are not ignored; there are only ten, but we have to use them all our lives, and we train the children to write them beautifully. It is marvelous what infants can do. Their English pronunciation is exactly like that of their American teacher. I listen to them enviously. But I have found that the most important thing is "memory talent education." The ability to memorize is one of the most vital skills and must be deeply inculcated.

In Daisetsu Suzuki's book *What is Zen?* he says: "One of the characteristics of human life is experience. That is because he [man] remembers. Memory is an extremely precious thing, and the fact that he speculates and conceives ideas is due to his having memory as a basis. Only because he has memory is experience possible, and if experience is possible, how many ways of evolution are open to him... . . With memory as the basis, he has experiences, and because of experience, he can reason."

So you see, memory is essential; depending on training, your ability to memorize gets better and better, and the time it takes to memorize gets shorter and shorter. You get so that you memorize immediately. And after you have learned something, you do not forget it. Memory skill can be acquired by anybody, if it is properly inculcated.

Children of high scholastic standing at school are simply ones whose memory skill is unusually well developed, and I believe that inferior students are merely ones who have not acquired memory skill. For essentially, all children have equal potential. In our infant school we train memory in the following way: they learn to recite haiku by Issa.

Since 1949, our Mrs. Yano has been working with new educational methods for developing ability, and every day she trains the infants of the school to memorize and recite Issa's well-known haiku.

Watching the results of this memory training over the past seventeen years, we have found that every one of the children had superior records at primary school.

Here is part of Mrs. Yano's training record in connection with Issa's haiku.

First term. 53 haiku, such as—
Melts the winter snow,
Melts, and now the turtledove
Sings upon a tree.

Melts the winter snow,
And the village now is full,
Full of children's glee.

Second term. 64 haiku, such as—
Hear the coltsfoot leaf
Splitting open with a pop.
Oh, how hot it is!

The little kitten, see,
Tries to catch between its paws
A falling autumn leaf.

Third term. 45 haiku, such as—
Crawling with a smile
Baby will be two years old
From this morning on.

Ah, my old home town.
Dumplings that they used to make,
Snow in springtime, too.

Children who at first could not memorize one haiku after hearing it ten times were able to do so in the second term after only three or four hearings, and in the third term only one hearing.

The haiku were selected for their interest, poetic charm, and observation of nature, as well as according to the season to make them easier to learn. At the end of the term all the students recite together the haiku they have learned that term. After training them like this every day, the children get so that they spontaneously make up their own haiku, expressing things they have noticed. Here are a few that either I or their parents wrote down—

At morn when I woke,
  In the washhand basin there
    Crawled a tiny snail.

Bicycling along,
  With a pink and frothy load of
    Cherry blossoms fair.

In the dark night sky,
  How they twinkle, how they shine
    All the little stars.

Wind-bells tinkling ring
  All the while my dear papa
    His siesta takes.

Jonquils growing fast,
  Getting taller every day
    Spring is born at last.

On the windowpane
  In the bathroom, crawls along
    one small garden snail.

When he wakes, each day,
  First he has to smoke his pipe,
    Dear old grandpapa.

Dahlias, big and round,
  Are they bigger than my face?
    No, they are not quite.

Pitter-pat it rains,
  And, alas, I cannot go
    out to romp and play.

Baby sparrows, see,
  At the lovely blossoms fair
    gaze in ecstasy.

These children do not forget their poetic skill, and when they get to primary school their teachers tell me they often add little haiku to the pictures they draw, and so on.

Well, I have given you some idea of the kind of training other than violin that we give to infants to develop their character. Now I shall tell you something about our violin training.

We encourage them to think of violin training as fun

Training the parent rather than the child. . . .

Although we accept infants, at first we do not have them play the violin. First we teach the mother to play one piece so that she will be a good teacher at home. As for the child, we first have him simply listen at home to a record of the piece he will be learning. Children are really educated in the home, so in order that the child will have good posture and practice properly at home, it is necessary for the parent to have firsthand experience. The correct education of the child depends on this. Until the parent can play one piece, the child does not play at all. This principle is very important indeed, because although the parent may want him to do so, a three- or four-year-old child has no desire to learn the violin. The idea is to get the child to say, "I want to play too"; so the first piece is played every day on the gramophone, and in the classroom he just watches the other children (and his mother) having their lessons. The proper environment is created for the child. The mother, moreover, both at home and in the classroom, plays on a small violin more suited to the child. The child will naturally before long take the violin away from his mother, thinking, "I want to play too." He knows the tune already. The other children are having fun; he wants to join in the fun. We have caused him to acquire this desire.

We encourage them to "play" with the violin

This situation having been created, lessons are led up to in the following order. First the parent asks, "Would you like to play the violin too?"

The answer is yes!

"You will practice hard?"

"Yes."

"All right; let's ask the teacher if you can join in next time."

This always succeeds. What a thrill the first private lesson always is! "I did it too," the child boasts. "Now I can play with the other children." Parents who understand children make fine teachers. In the classroom there are private lessons and group lessons. Parents who do not understand children think they are paying for the private lessons and that the group lessons are just recreation periods. So although they make sure that their children attend the private lessons, they often fail to bring them to the group lessons. But the fact is that what the children enjoy most is the group playing. They play with children who are more advanced than they are; the influence is enormous and is marvelous for their training. This is the real talent education.

A game to begin with, the spirit of fun leads them on

"My child doesn't like to practice at home," complain quite a few parents. It is because they do not understand the mind of a child who thinks that the violin is fun. Parents of this sort resent paying good money just to have the child think it is a mere game. In other words, they are calculating about education, and their attitude discourages the children. Starting children off with the fun of playing a game, letting their spirit of fun lead them in the right direction, is the way all education of children should be started.

Hitomi Kasuya was three and would play the violin for three hours every day. How could a three-year-old do that? Hitomi's mother bought her a violin instead of a doll and played a record of the piece to be studied over and over again as a kind of background music. Hitomi played with the violin all day, as if it were a toy. Her mother would now and then show her the correct way to play, according to our instructions, letting Hitomi think she was playing a game with her. This is the art of education at its best. The thing that matters is the result: that the child acquires the skill. If you are formal and strict and have a "this-is-education" attitude, you will immediately warp the child. First you must educate the mind, then inculcate the skill. This is a correct, natural method. Hitomi Kasuya developed rapidly with this method, and in 1964, when she was five, she took her little violin and went to America with us.

Five minutes every day versus three hours every day

In contrast to children who do not like to practice at home there are plenty of examples of children to whom violin practice becomes a natural event of the day, because of the wise lead of their mothers.

One year at summer school I noticed a six-year-old playing the Vivaldi concerto with fine style and tone. I asked the mother how long the child had been playing.

"One year and a half."

"How well she plays! How long does she practice every day?"

"About three hours."

That was what I had thought. A child who practices well shows it in his playing. You can tell immediately. Practicing according to the correct method and practicing as much as possible is the way to acquire ability. If one is faithful to the principle, superior skill develops without fail. If you compare a person who practices five minutes a day with one who practices three hours a day, the difference, even though they both practice daily, is enormous. Those who fail to practice sufficiently fail to acquire ability. Only the effort that is actually expended will bear results. There is no shortcut. If the five-minute-a-day person wants to accomplish what the three-hour-a-day person does, it will take him nine years. What one accomplishes in three months will take the other nine years. There is no reason why it should be otherwise. Hitomi Kasuya, Toshiya Eto, Koji Toyoda, and Kenji Kobayashi all practiced three hours a day and more.

The development of ability is through the right kind of practice

For someone to complain, "But I studied for five years," means nothing. It all depends on how much he did each day. "I spent five years on it," someone says. But five minutes a day for five years is only 150 hours. What that person should have said is, "I did it for 150 hours and I'm still no better." That makes some sense. It is no wonder he got no better. To put your talent up on the shelf and then say you were born without any is utter nonsense.

The development of ability is straightforward. This can be absolutely relied upon. People either become experts at doing the right thing, which is seen as a fine talent, or they become experts at doing something wrong and unacceptable, which is seen as lack of talent. So it behooves everyone to become expert in the right things, and the more training he or she receives the better. Depending on these two things—practice and practice of the right things—superior ability can be produced in anyone. For twenty years I have watched with my own eyes the education of thousands of children, as well as the effect on them of the superiority or inferiority of their parents and teachers, and I can say without any hesitation whatsoever that this is true.

The first piece that the infants learn to play is "Variations on 'Twinkle, Twinkle, Little Star.'" After having heard the record daily at home, they learn to play it themselves. The lessons are given with infinite care. As soon as they can play the piece, they are told, "Now we are going to learn how to do it beautifully." This is a very important step and aims at the improvement of quality. It is the beginning of lessons designed to produce finer tone quality, more graceful movement, greater accuracy, and better musicianship. We educate their talent using this piece as the teaching material. And every child, without exception, learns to play it magnificently. Their tone gradually improves, their movements become free and graceful, and they become fine musicians. Talent has been inculcated in them.

I firmly believe that any child can become superior, and my confidence has never been shaken. I am determined that each and every child shall become superior, for if one does not I consider it a personal failure that I cannot condone. I test the children to find out how much they have so far acquired of the ability that is being inculcated in them. In order to do this I play games with them.

"How many legs have you?"

When the children have learned how to play "Twinkle, Twinkle, Little Star" variations easily and freely, I ask them to play them, and I say, "Now let's play a game. I want you to answer my questions while you go on playing. Answer in a loud voice, and don't stop playing." Then, in a loud voice, I call out, "How many legs have you?" They think this is loads of fun, and answer all together at the top of their voices, "Two." Now, if they can do this while playing correctly, it means that the skill has been properly inculcated and has become second nature. If, among them, there is a child for whom it is not yet second nature, he will be so intent on his playing that he does not reply. Or if he replies, he will stop playing. I ask many different questions and they answer while playing. Smiling sweetly, they have acquired the ability to play games with me while they go on playing the violin. Every single child, without fail, gets so he can do this. We are able to do all sorts of tasks while we are speaking in Japanese because it is second nature. It is exactly the same with the violin.

There are several other test games, and I often try them to find out how much proficiency they have attained and how much their power of intuition has developed. I try these on ten or fifteen children at once, or, if there is enough space, forty or fifty. Another thing I do is to play the first part of a piece in mime only, with empty hands. I play it only once. Then I say, "Get set—go." Having carefully watched my movements, they play the piece with one accord. This is the way we train them to be quick and alert and develop their intuitive power.

As the children become more advanced, so do the test games. Those games are designed to test their developing powers of intuition as well as to educate their ability still further. If this real ability and the vital power of intuition is developed so that they become a power that is unrestricted and second nature, the child will eventually find that this helps him to acquire greater skill in any sphere of activity.

We amaze the world

More than twenty years have passed since Violin Talent Education for infants was started. Now in Japan, children from the age of three or four, using tiny violins, develop high sensibility and noble-mindedness through the music of Bach and Mozart. Over 200,000 children have already taken this course. Nowhere in the world can such a thing be equaled. Father Candeau, a Catholic priest, who died in 1953, was greatly moved by one of the mass concerts given by a thousand children at the Tokyo Gymnasium, and said, "A miracle has come to pass."

Today people throughout the world express great interest and amazement at this thing that is happening in Japan.

This is the true face of youth

Georges Duhamel (1884–1966), was not only a poet but a dramatist, novelist, and critic, as well as one of France's most representative men of letters. In 1953, eight years after the Talent Education movement started, he came to Japan and heard a violin performance by the children of the Nagoya branch, which is led by Professor Nishizaki. After hearing these children, Duhamel wrote an article entitled "Ideal Childhood," whose gist is as follows:

> If I had to advise travellers to Japan and those who attempt to criticize Japan, the first thing I would say is: go to Nagoya. Why? Because I found something there that is quite astonishing. After a lunch in the restaurant of Nagoya's Asahi Kaikan, I listened to about 30 children playing the violin all together. When I first saw these boys and girls aged 6 to 10 coming out with their tiny violins, I thought this must be some childish game. But, led by a young conductor, they proceeded to play a Vivaldi concerto. And what a really superb performance it was. I was not only moved, I was entranced.
>
> This, indeed, was the ideal manifestation of childhood. To tell you the truth, I have never seen children before in my life who have displayed such fine musical technique.
>
> The children played Bach with innocent expression on their faces, but their polyphony had all the required accuracy and refinement. It was a most difficult feat, but the children accomplished it splendidly. And then the best player among them, a tiny girl, played a piece by Mozart with artistic fervour and superb style. This piece is not an easy one even for experts, and she played it accurately and beautifully. Moreover, in the city of Nagoya alone, there are several hundred of these little violinists playing difficult polyphonic music.

As a traveller from western Europe, I thought the almost too precocious display of talent by these small children was quite extraordinary, but at the same time I was reminded of the sense of tradition that lies at the heart of the Japanese people. In spite of their handicap of being oriental, and Japanese, these children have been trained to reach heights only attained by the most superior children in Europe. From my point of view Japan is the Far West, not the Far East. I unhesitatingly say, The Japanese, among the peoples of the Orient, are the most European race.

Casals wept

In 1961, eight years after Duhamel's visit, on April 16 at ten o'clock, four hundred children aged five to twelve stood in neat rows on the stage of Tokyo's Bunkyo Hall with small violins in their hands. The children were waiting for the arrival of one of the twentieth century's greatest cellists, Pablo Casals. The great maestro's car reached the entrance of the hall at two minutes to ten. And at ten o'clock sharp Maestro and Mrs. Casals came into the hall, to be greeted by the enthusiastic applause of the children's parents as well as of teachers of the Talent Education movement. As soon as he came in, and saw the four hundred children lined up on the stage, he said, "Oh . . .oh," greatly moved, and he and Mrs. Casals both waved their hands to the children and then sat down. They were no sooner seated when all the children on stage started playing "Twinkle, Twinkle, Little Star" variations in unison. It was a lively performance by the four hundred children. "Oh...oh," the old maestro said again, following the performance throughout with deep emotion. His excitement reached its peak when the children played the Vivaldi concerto and then the Bach concerto for two violins. The maestro was weeping. His eyes were filled with tears, and his mouth was twisted with emotion. And when fifteen or sixteen children, who had been taught the cello by Yoshio Sato, a pupil of Casals', played Saint-Saëns' "Swan" and Bach's "Bourree," the great teacher's emotion knew no bounds.

When the children's performance was over, I went to Casals to thank him for having listened to them, but before I could finish, he threw both his arms around me and silently wept on my shoulder.

How often I myself had wept at this beautiful, innocent outpouring of the children's inner life force! Now the great seventy-five-year-old maestro himself was speechless in this sublime moment before the sound of that life force. Mr. and Mrs. Casals then went up on the stage, patting the heads of the children as they moved to the center of the stage. Chairs had been put there for them. Holding the bouquet of flowers that the children had presented to them, they sat down. Surrounded by these sweet little Japanese children, and in a voice shaking with emotion, the maestro spoke into the microphone—

> Ladies and gentlemen, I assist to one of the most moving scenes that one can see. What we are contemplating has much more importance than it seems. I don't think that in any country in the world we could feel such spirit of fraternity or cordiality in its utmost. I feel in every moment that I have had the privilege of living in this country such proof of heart, of desire of a better world. And this is what has impressed me most in this country. The superlative desire of the highest things in life and how wonderful is to see that the grown-up people think of the smallest like this as to teach them to begin with the noble feelings, with the noble deeds. And one of this music. To train them to music to make them understand that music is not only sound to have to dance or to have small pleasure, but such a high thing in life that perhaps it is music that will save the world.
>
> Now, I not only congratulate you, the teachers, the grown-up people, but I want to say: my whole admiration, my whole respect and my heartiest congratulations. And another thing that I am happy to say at this moment is that Japan is a great people, and Japan is not only great by its deeds in industrial, in science, in art, but Japan is, I would say, the heart of the heart, and this is what humanity needs first, first, first.

In America, the expanding Talent Education Movement takes hold

Without my realizing it, the movement had become a sensation in America, where it now is being more and more widely accepted and on a greater scale than in Japan. Ten years before I heard about him, Mr. Mochizuki, who was the Japanese Consulate General in New York, had known about Talent Education, ever since he was at Oberlin (Ohio) College. He became determined to plant the seed in America and informed me so in a letter. Being successful in obtaining a copy of a seven-minute film that had once been taken at a Tokyo annual concert of the children playing Bach's Double Violin Concerto, he showed this film, with the permission of Professor Cook, at Oberlin College. This was the spark that set the Talent Education movement going in America. The first people to take action were Professor Kendall of the music department of Muskingum College (Ohio) and Professor Clifford Cook of Oberlin. In 1959, Mr. Kendall came to Japan for an inspection and observation tour, and stayed in Matsumoto for a month, after which he returned home and published my violin method, as well as giving lectures all over America, spreading the Talent Education method. Later, Mr. Cook toured Japan and spent a long time in Matsumoto doing research. Now many young students are being successfully educated in the Oberlin College Talent Education Workshop.

In 1961, Mr. Mochizuki wrote to me, "Now I shall do my best to get you to come to America."

Performances and lectures in sixteen cities

In America it was thought that children could not and would not study the violin until they were eight or nine years old. So you can imagine their astonishment when they saw with their own eyes eight hundred Japanese children, including some only three to five years old, playing Bach's difficult Double Violin Concerto. By 1965 our annual All-Japan String Concert had been shown on European television. Koji Toyoda wrote from Berlin that people who saw the performance by eighteen hundred children on television "were astonished and could not believe it to be true."

In 1964, we toured America with a party of nineteen, giving concerts and lectures. The ten students were aged five to thirteen. We had been invited by the American String Teachers Association. We spent two weeks in America and flew over the whole country, visiting universities in sixteen cities and giving twenty-six concerts and lectures. We were constantly on the move. The children I took along came from Nagano and Aichi prefectures as well as Tokyo, and had been assembled with regard only to their ability to be away at that time and not musical consideration. I had intended to rehearse them en route, but there was no time for anything like that. As a result, children who had never seen one another before had to line up together on the stage without a single rehearsal. Every evening's performance was televised. We caused a tremendous sensation in America.

The first concert, at Washington University, was more like a rehearsal than anything else, but as concert followed concert the children began to perform spendidly. Soon after the beginning of each concert the audience would bring out handkerchiefs to mop their eyes. After the concert they would come backstage; even mothers with children had tears in their eyes.

"Fiddling legions"

Under this title *Newsweek* of March 25, 1964, wrote as follows about the concerts of the Japanese children in America:

> Seven-year-old Asako Hata playfully dropped a chunk of ice down her neighbor's back, and the long table of children at lunch one day last week burst into delighted giggles. Forty minutes later, Asako was standing on the stage of New York's august Juilliard School of Music, bobbing her head shyly to acknowledge the thunderous clapping that greeted her performance of a complicated Veracini sonata. The solo climaxed a concert that was at once impressive and absurd, in which ten tiny Japanese children, ranging in age 5 to 14 played Bach and Vivaldi that drew bravos from a highly critical audience of Juilliard students and faculty. If their applause was tinged with sentimentality (when the children's teacher, Professor Shinichi Suzuki, stepped on stage to tune a 5-year-old's quarter-size violin, the audience sighed), it was nonetheless wholly deserved. "This is amazing," said Juilliard violin Professor Ivan Galamian. "They show remarkable training, a wonderful feeling for the rhythm and flow of music."

Playing without a conductor and using no scores, the youngsters were a living testimonial to the validity of Suzuki's unorthodox teaching method. He starts his children about 3, but the first lessons are for the child's mother. She comes once a week with her youngster, and after three months has normally progressed to "Twinkle, Twinkle, Little Star." "By that time," Suzuki explains in a mixture of German and English as expressive as his face, "the child has watched the mother play and wants to imitate her." Only then is the pupil given a pint-size violin. Through exposure to classical recordings and constant repetition, the child is ready to tackle simple Bach gavottes within a year. The 150,000 children Suzuki's system has trained in 30 years are far from robots. They combine virtuosity with feeling so successfully that when Pablo Casals heard a Suzuki recital in Tokyo, he rushed to the stage, shouting "bravo," and hugged the children.

SENSITIVITY

Although about 5 percent of Suzuki's students make careers in music, the 65-year-old professor insists: "I just want to make good citizens. If a child hears good music from the day of his birth, and learns to play it himself, he develops sensitivity, discipline and endurance. He gets a beautiful heart." Suzuki thoughtfully crinkled a few of the paper-wrapped candies he carries for his musicians. "If nations cooperate in raising good children, perhaps there won't be any war."

Suzuki has done more than revolutionize violin teaching in Japan. Oberlin Professor Clifford Cook says: *"What Suzuki has done for young children earns him a place among the benefactors of mankind, along with Schweitzer, Casals, and Tom Dooley."**

POSTSCRIPT

My dream for the happiness of all people

I feel respect and friendly feelings for everyone. In particular I cannot help but feel respect and warm friendship for small children. And my heart brims over with a desire to help make all the children born upon this earth fine human beings, happy people, people of superior ability. My whole life and energies and devoted to this end. This is because of my discovery that every single child, without exception, is born with this possibility.

People say that I am trying to do the impossible, and expending my energies for nothing. But I know that what I conceive *is* possible, and I believe that one day the human race will create the kind of world in which everyone will realize that children have the potential. That is why at the United Nations, after Casals had spoken on world peace, I appealed to the representatives of the nations of the world to do something. What I am trying to do now is to apply my Talent Education to all areas of life. I am trying to get sympathetic primary-school principals to try out methods of education that will ensure that not even one student fails in school. I am also trying to get something done about mentally retarded children, and to persuade sympathetic politicians to clarify national policy with regard to children.

To make my dream not just a dream but a reality is my earnest prayer

If the world finally lives up to the Children's Charter, which states that all children must be cared for, then my dream will not have

been just a dream. This task is an extremely important one for all
of us on this globe.

A real children's charter is needed that provides care and education for every single baby that is born. This was my earnest prayer
as I started the Talent Education movement. Many babies who could
have been educated failed to be educated on account of poverty. But
there is also failure due to bad educational methods. It should be
the responsibility of the state to see that this does not happen.

Just as a policeman has his beat, which he is responsible for and
patrols, probation officers for infants should be trained by the state,
and should be stationed throughout Japan to be responsible for child
training in each home. The state should spare no energy in seeing
that children of preschool age develop along the right lines.

I believe that those reading this book will have seen what superior
human beings children can become, depending on their training as
infants. To apply the old Japanese proverb "What he is at three he
will be at a hundred" to a child whose character is already molded
is merely irresponsible. A child of three—in other words, an infant—
is just at the stage when his personality is being formed and his
abilities are being inculcated. Consequently, I believe that this is the
crucial time, when a child's character and abilities can easily be
damaged and warped. It is precisely at this time that he must be
educated with infinite care, and the state should realize what an important long-term project this is for the future of the country.

Not tomorrow but right now, today

People today are like gardeners who look sadly at ruined sap-
lings and shake their heads, saying the seeds must have been bad
to start with, not realizing that the seed was all right, but that their
method of cultivation was wrong. They go on in their mistaken way,
ruining plant after plant. It is imperative that the human race escape
from this vicious circle. The sooner people realize their mistake, the
better. The more the situation is changed, the nearer the human race
will come to happiness.

I too am one of those people whose early life was damaged by
the wrong kind of education. Most people could say the same. I have

tried to remedy this, and from the time I was young, I have been working hard trying to improve myself.

I sincerely hope that readers of this book will realize from all I have said that there is no need for any of us to despair. We are all born with a high potential, and if we try hard we can all become superior human beings and acquire talent and ability.

If you have really understood my message, you will not put it off until tomorrow, but will put it into action right now, today. And your life will become happier as a result. That this may become true for everyone is my heartfelt dream.